Thomas Aschauer

Framework Design Pattern Annotation

Thomas Aschauer

Framework Design Pattern Annotation

Implementation and Application of the UML-F Profile for Framework Architectures

VDM Verlag Dr. Müller

Impressum/Imprint (nur für Deutschland/ only for Germany)

Bibliografische Information der Deutschen Nationalbibliothek: Die Deutsche Nationalbibliothek verzeichnet diese Publikation in der Deutschen Nationalbibliografie; detaillierte bibliografische Daten sind im Internet über http://dnb.d-nb.de abrufbar.

Alle in diesem Buch genannten Marken und Produktnamen unterliegen warenzeichen-, marken- oder patentrechtlichem Schutz bzw. sind Warenzeichen oder eingetragene Warenzeichen der jeweiligen Inhaber. Die Wiedergabe von Marken, Produktnamen, Gebrauchsnamen, Handelsnamen, Warenbezeichnungen u.s.w. in diesem Werk berechtigt auch ohne besondere Kennzeichnung nicht zu der Annahme, dass solche Namen im Sinne der Warenzeichen- und Markenschutzgesetzgebung als frei zu betrachten wären und daher von jedermann benutzt werden dürften.

Coverbild: www.purestockx.com

Verlag: VDM Verlag Dr. Müller Aktiengesellschaft & Co. KG
Dudweiler Landstr. 125 a, 66123 Saarbrücken, Deutschland
Telefon +49 681 9100-698, Telefax +49 681 9100-988, Email: info@vdm-verlag.de

Herstellung in Deutschland:
Schaltungsdienst Lange o.H.G., Zehrensdorfer Str. 11, D-12277 Berlin
Books on Demand GmbH, Gutenbergring 53, D-22848 Norderstedt
Reha GmbH, Dudweiler Landstr. 99, D- 66123 Saarbrücken
ISBN: 978-3-639-05081-3

Imprint (only for USA, GB)

Bibliographic information published by the Deutsche Nationalbibliothek: The Deutsche Nationalbibliothek lists this publication in the Deutsche Nationalbibliografie; detailed bibliographic data are available in the Internet at http://dnb.d-nb.de.

Any brand names and product names mentioned in this book are subject to trademark, brand or patent protection and are trademarks or registered trademarks of their respective holders. The use of brand names, product names, common names, trade names, product descriptions etc. even without
a particular marking in this works is in no way to be construed to mean that such names may be regarded as unrestricted in respect of trademark and brand protection legislation and could thus be used by anyone.

Cover image: www.purestockx.com

Publisher:
VDM Verlag Dr. Müller Aktiengesellschaft & Co. KG
Dudweiler Landstr. 125 a, 66123 Saarbrücken, Germany
Phone +49 681 9100-698, Fax +49 681 9100-988, Email: info@vdm-verlag.de

Produced in USA and UK by:
Lightning Source Inc., 1246 Heil Quaker Blvd., La Vergne, TN 37086, USA
Lightning Source UK Ltd., Chapter House, Pitfield, Kiln Farm, Milton Keynes, MK11 3LW, GB
BookSurge, 7290 B. Investment Drive, North Charleston, SC 29418, USA
ISBN: 978-3-639-05081-3

Contents

III   PANEX at Work — Case Studies   133

IV   Appendix   169

In the last decades, as software systems became larger and increasingly complex, the benefits of software reuse have been recognized and exploited by industry and academia. Design patterns, providing means for reusing software design knowledge, capture the context and the structure of recurring problems that arise in the engineering and development of software. Design patterns also provide hints and proposals for solutions to these problems, and they form a common body of design knowledge that helps to communicate ideas among peer developers efficiently. Frameworks are reusable software architectures that allow the reuse of design models, of code, and of valuable domain expertise.

Visual modeling is one of the key aspects of modern software development. The Unified Modeling Language provides notions for representing software models in a graphical notation. When a design pattern is applied in the design of a framework architecture and when the pattern is composed with other patterns, however, some of the related information may be lost because traditional UML diagrams do not track this information. As a consequence, it becomes hard for a framework user to identify the design patterns underlying the framework design. This information is of great value since it efficiently communicates the framework developer's basic intents, and usually also highlights the framework variation points. Thus, adequate framework documentation demands for more sophisticated representations of design patterns than provided by the standard UML notation.

UML profiles are extensions to the basic language for the purpose of customizing the UML for the specific needs of certain application domains. The *UML Profile for Framework Architectures* (*UML-F*) is an extension that allows for the depiction of framework variation points by documenting the design patterns and *essential construction principles* applied in a framework's design. Tags that indicate pattern roles enrich the UML design diagrams for the purpose of highlighting variation points implemented by design patterns, thus clarifying the framework design. In this book, an updated version of the UML-F profile that is compatible to UML 2 is presented.

Adequate tool support is needed in real-world framework development projects for such an extension to be of value to the framework developer and to the application developer using the framework. The overhead of creating diagrams that describe design pattern usage has to be as small as possible compared to the creation of standard UML design diagrams. Also a clear and intuitive notation has to be supported to get readable diagrams that can be understood quickly by all potential framework users, not just by distinguished experts.

The *PANEX* tool, whose development is documented in this book, provides the required support for the *UML Profile for Framework Architectures*. It is designed as plug-in to an open source UML tool and provides functionality for annotating design models with tags that correspond to the pattern roles of the design patterns used. In addition, annotated diagrams can be generated at different levels of abstractions, ranging from abstract construction principles for reusable object-oriented software to highly specialized domain specific design patterns.

Book Structure

This book is divided into of four parts. Part one, *Design Pattern Annotation*, is the introductory part. In the first chapter the concepts of design patterns and frameworks are introduced. The second chapter briefly introduces the Unified Modeling Language, and the UML-F profile is presented as an extension to UML 2. Finally, the requirements for a tool supporting the UML-F approach are stated.

The second part, *A Vision Becomes Reality*, documents the development of the PANEX tool. First, the requirements analysis for a tool supporting the UML-F profile is presented. Second, the decision for a certain UML tool as basis for the development is explained in detail. Third, the software design is presented and the problems that arose during the tool development are described together with their solutions.

Part three, *ArgoUML Featuring PANEX*, contains two case studies that show the usability of the tool and the appropriateness of the annotated design diagrams that can be generated automatically. In addition, a discussion of related approaches for depicting pattern roles in UML diagrams is given. Concluding remarks round out the third part.

The fourth part is the appendix, containing a reference chapter for the pattern library developed for the PANEX tool, several indices, a glossary, and the bibliography.

Acknowledgements

First and foremost I would like to express my sincere gratitude and appreciation to Prof. Wolfgang Pree for his guidance, feedback and encouragement.
I am especially grateful to my specific other, Astrid, for her love, encouragement, and understanding.
Last but not least, I would like to thank my lovely parents and my sister Barbara for their help and support.

Pischelsdorf, Austria, March 2005

Revised Edition

This book is a revised edition of my master thesis "Design Pattern Annotation in a UML-Tool", which I prepared at the University of Salzburg's Department of Computer Sciences in 2005.

Salzburg, Austria, September 2008

x _____

Part I

Design Pattern Annotation

Introduction and Theoretical Foundations to Design
Pattern Annotation for Framework Documentation

CHAPTER 1

Knowledge, Reuse and Patterns: A Software Engineer's Toolbox

Computer science researchers are constantly looking for new ways to improve the state-of-the-art of software engineering. Improving the quality of software products and increasing the productivity of software engineers are two important reasons.

First steps towards increasing a programmer's productivity were achieved by using higher levels of abstraction, i.e. by using higher programming languages, and by developing appropriate tool support such as compilers.

In the pioneering days of computer science, the term *software engineering* was first coined by F.L. Bauer at a meeting of the NATO Science Committee in Brussels 1967: *"The whole trouble comes from the fact that there is so much tinkering with software. It is not made in a clean fabrication process, which it should be. [...] What we need is 'software engineering'."* [Bau93]. The first conference on that topic, also organized by the NATO Science Committee, was held in Garmisch, Germany, in 1968 [NR69]. At about that time, the need for structure and modularity was stated by prominent authors. First solutions on how to deal with the complexity in large software projects[1], but also with the problem of multiple program versions throughout the whole product live cycle were proposed, for instance, in the groundbreaking papers of Dijkstra [Dij70] and Parnas [Par72].

As software systems became larger and increasingly complex, the benefits of software reuse

---

[1] *Large* in this context is meant in the sense of Dijkstra [Dij70, p. 84]: *"... programs that are large due to the complexity of their task, in contrast to programs that have exploded (by inadequacy of the equipment, unhappy decisions, poor understanding of the problem, etc.)"*.

gained on importance. The software engineering community has been applying several reuse techniques based on the object-technology (OT) paradigm, ranging from early class and component libraries to recent reusable architectures, also known as *frameworks*, and *design patterns*.

This chapter introduces design patterns and framework architectures as two techniques that are valuable to software engineers for the development of large systems.

1.1 Patterns – Reusing Knowledge and Experience

Senior software engineers often solve a problem or parts of it by applying a solution they already have applied in another context or they have seen earlier. They use their experience and knowledge to *reapply* a particular solution idea to the given problem in order to construct a new solution. These solutions, how they work out and which problems they bring along is a significant part of their expert repertoire. Furthermore, the knowledge of the ramifications a solution implies builds the logical foundation for these experts to explain why certain solutions are appropriate in a given context or why certain solutions do not work.

Patterns generalize and formalize the process of finding a solution by means of earlier solutions to similar problems. For a particular solution that has been applied several times, the concrete problem structure is abstracted and the solution is given a descriptive name. The solution's strategy is stated in a way that makes it easy to be applied to any problem with a similar structure. Such a description, dedicated to the field of software design, is called a *design pattern*. A match in the problem structure, however, is not sufficient for the applicability of a certain pattern. The contextual domain, the solution structure and many other consequences have to be taken into consideration, too. Design pattern descriptions usually are enriched by discussions of these aspects.

Algorithms are procedures to solve computational problems. Patterns also are proven solutions to recurring problems, however, they are more than just algorithms and heuristics: commonly they are supported by a rationale and put into a certain context [App98]. Algorithms frequently are employed in the implementation of a pattern, but they are only one part of a pattern. Typically they solve more fine-grained problems like searching and sorting, while patterns are concerned with broader architectural issues.

Pattern catalogs are collections of design patterns that have proven their applicability in a certain application domain. The most famous pattern catalog nowadays is that of Gamma et al. [GHJV95]. The catalog, which is also referred to as the *Gang of Four (GoF) catalog*, lists 23 patterns of general purpose in the domains of object creation, structural decomposition and behavior. Buschmann et al. [BMR⁺96] also present a catalog of general purpose design patterns, however, the focus is on architectural and structural patterns. An example of a pattern catalog that documents well known solutions for one specific application domain is published by Alur et al. [AMC01]: the catalog contains patterns for web-applications in the context of the *Java 2 Enterprise Edition* (*J2EE*) environment.

Patterns and catalogs of patterns turned out to be very useful in various ways: they build the basis for knowledge transfer, since the experience and knowledge of one or more experts is extracted and documented in a written form. Moreover, they provide a common vocabulary for software designers. Designers can use the pattern names for efficient communication because they describe concepts that are on high level of abstraction. Patterns also prevent from *reinventing the wheel*. That is, one can consult pattern catalogs to find a solution for a particular problem situation. In the usual case this is faster than inventing a new solution from scratch, in particular if the designer already has intimate knowledge of patterns. When a pattern is chosen from a catalog, the resulting consequences and ramifications are well documented, which is rarely the case for new solutions. Very often they are not understood well, either due to lack of experience or simply because of limited time. Even if the software engineers are aware of these aspects, in most cases they are not documented explicitly.

1.1.1 Construction Principles for Reusable Object-Oriented Software

One reason for the widespread use of the object-oriented paradigm nowadays is its contribution to the manageability of the complexity of large software systems. This is achieved through the OO-concepts of *information hiding* and *encapsulation*. Another reason for this paradigm's success is the high adaptability and flexibility of object-oriented software, which is realized through the mechanisms of *inheritance*, *polymorphism* and *dynamic binding*. All these concepts are integral concepts of modern object-oriented programming languages.

Callback-Style of Programming

Reusability in object-oriented software programs is achieved through the *callback-style of programming* [PP04, chapter 5]. The basic idea of that programming technique, which has been used in the procedural programming paradigm for decades, is the use of a function or procedure as a parameter.[2] When the parameterized function is executed (this function is called *template function*), it calls the parameter function, which conforms to a predefined interface and performs a certain task. The parameter function is called *hook function*. The template function's

---

[2]For the purpose of this chapter it is not necessary to distinguish between functions and procedures, and thus the two terms are used synonymously.

hook parameter can be modified, i.e. a different hook function is set as parameter, in order to change the template function's execution semantics. An example is a template function that implements a sorting algorithm, and the ordering scheme is encapsulated as the call of a hook function. Several different hook functions can implement the required ordering schemes, for instance the lexicographic ordering.

To apply the idea of the callback-style of programming to object-orientation, both the template function and the hook function have to be implemented as methods of classes. The adaptation process is realized by inheritance. In other words, the template method either calls an abstract hook method or it calls a default implementation, while adaptation is done by overriding the hook method. The hook method does not necessarily have to be defined in the same class as the template method; the template method also can use a parameter object that contains the hook method. Recursive combinations of template and hook methods also can be implemented. Table 1.1 gives an overview of possible combinations, which will be discussed in detail in the subsequent sections:

Construction Principle	Hook Location	Recursive Combination	Multiplicity (Parent – Child)
Hook Method	Same Class as Template	No	—
Hook Object	Separate Class	No	—
Chain-Of-Responsibility	Hook = Template	Yes	1 – 0..1
Composite	Separate Class	Yes	1 – 0..*
Decorator	Separate Class	Yes	1 – 1

Table 1.1: Template-Hook combinations of essential construction principles

Hook-Method

The *Hook-Method*[3] construction principle is, compared to the other essential construction principles, the simplest but also the least flexible one. Figure 1.1 on the next page shows the principle's basic structure.

Both, the template method and the hook method, are located in the same class. Inheritance can be used to modify the behavior by subclassing HookMethod-TH and overriding the hook method. If a default implementation of the hook method is not provided, it is declared as an abstract method.

---

[3]Earlier publications called this construction principle the *Unification* principle. This was due to the intention of the principle to unite hook and template in the same class. See, for example, Fontoura et al. [FPR01]. The recent terminology was introduced by Pomberger and Pree [PP04].

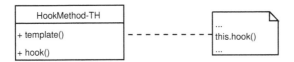

Figure 1.1: Hook-Method structure

Hook-Object

Figure 1.2 shows the basic structure of the *Hook-Object*[4] construction principle.

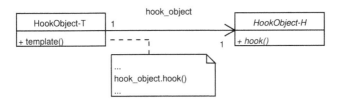

Figure 1.2: Hook-Object structure

The template method and the hook method are located in separate classes. Flexibility is achieved by the combination of inheritance with object composition: to customize the behavior of the template class *HookObject-T*, a subclass of the abstract class *HookObject-H* has to implement the **hook** method and the **template-field** has to reference an instance of the subclass. Several different *hook objects* can be *plugged* into the *template object* at runtime, thus offering greater flexibility than the Hook-Method principle. Note that supporting methods, such as a setter method for **template-field**, are not part of the diagram for the purpose brevity.

Chain-Of-Responsibility

The *Chain-Of-Responsibility* construction principle (the corresponding acronym is *COR*) is a recursive construction principle with a simple structure, as shown in figure 1.3 on the next page.

The COR construction principle basically manages a chain that can grow and shrink dynamically at runtime. Messages or message objects are routed along the chain by the chain elements

---

[4]This principle was called the *Separation* principle in earlier publications, since the basic idea is to separate hook and template into two different classes. The recent terminology was introduced by Pomberger and Pree [PP04].

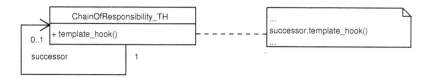

Figure 1.3: Chain-Of-Responsibility structure

themselves. If a certain chain element is interested in a particular message, i.e. it is a *sink* for the message, it performs the corresponding action and can decide to continue the routing by sending the message to the next chain element.

Static adaptation can be achieved by creating subclasses of ChainOfResponsibility_TH and overriding the template_hook method. The power of this principle originates from the flexibility to combine and recombine chain elements dynamically. Methods that are required for chain management, for instance a method set_successor for passing chain elements the reference to the succeeding chain element, are omitted in the class diagram of figure 1.3.

Composite

The structure of the *Composite* construction principle is depicted in figure 1.4. This construction principle is used to represent *part-whole hierarchies*, which typically form tree structures.

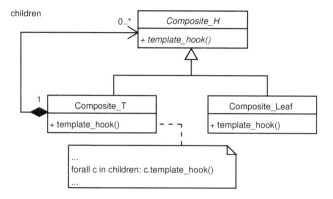

Figure 1.4: Composite structure

Composite_H declares the interface for all objects in the composition and, if applicable, implements the common behavior. If there is no meaningful default implementation, the hook class *Composite_H* can be represented by an interface. Different composition node behaviors can be implemented in subclasses of the hook class. These classes are either template classes or leaf classes. Template classes, represented by Composite_T in the class diagram, are composition elements that have children. Leaf classes, represented by Composite_Leaf in the class diagram, are composition elements without children. Template classes are responsible for traversing the tree structure in a recursive manner, which is depicted by the note in the class diagram.

Management methods, such as a method add_child for building the tree, are not shown in the class diagram.

Decorator

Another recursive template-hook combination is the *Decorator* construction principle, which is used to adapt the behavior of an existing object. The class diagram shown in figure 1.5 depicts the principle's basic structure. The main difference between the Decorator principle and the previously discussed principles is that here the hook is considered to be fixed, while the template is used to obtain dynamic flexibility.

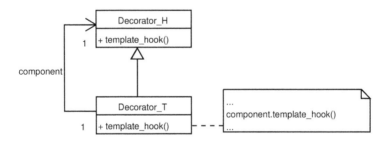

Figure 1.5: Decorator structure

The class to be adapted, Decorator_H, represents the hook class. To adapt the behavior, the class Decorator_T, also known as *decorator*, is created as subclass of Decorator_H, and all methods of Decorator_H are overridden. Template methods that do not provide additional functionality to the corresponding hook method simply forward the message. Altered behavior is achieved by template methods that call the corresponding hook object's methods and also perform specific tasks.

The power of this concept stems from the independence of different decorators and their possible combinations. Let there be one hook and three decorators. Then there are six possible ways to *decorate* the hook class. Obviously, the same effect can be achieved by using inheritance, but to achieve the same number of different behaviors, six subclasses are needed. For large class hierarchies, where the behavior of one of the base classes has to be adapted, applying the Decorator principle can significantly reduce the required effort compared to using inheritance only.

The Decorator principle usually is used together with a Composite implementation. The Decorator approach also has been applied successfully for altering the behavior of class library members whose source code is not available.

1.1.2   Design Pattern Catalog

Gamma et al. [GHJV95] present a catalog of 23 design patterns. Design patterns are more specific than essential construction principles. They describe design solutions based on a *problem — solution* approach using collections of classes and objects. In contrast, the essential construction principles describe how the basic mechanisms of object-orientation can be used to create flexible object structures.

Catalog entries comprise four essential elements:

Pattern name: A meaningful name, i.e. a single word or a short phrase, which defines the handle that can be used to refer to the problem description, its solution, and consequences. Introduction of pattern names enriches the design vocabulary, thus enabling designers to communicate in an efficient way because of the high level of abstraction.

Problem: The description of the pattern's intent, that is, the goals that have to be reached within the given context. The problem statement sometimes includes a description of preconditions that must be met for an application of the pattern to be reasonable.

Solution: Describes the elements that are part of the design solution, their static structure and their dynamic behavior. The description is presented in an abstract way in order to ease the application to a wide variety of concrete problem situations. It may encompass diagrams and prose specifying the pattern's participants, their relationships, collaborations and responsibilities.

Consequences: Discusses the resulting design, its ramifications, advantages and trade-offs. This includes descriptions of problems that may arise from the application of the pattern and its impact on a system's flexibility, extensibility, or portability. The *consequences* part is essential for an efficient evaluation of different design pattern alternatives in a concrete problem situation.

The catalog is organized according to the problem domains the entries are related to. *Creational patterns* are concerned with the abstraction of the instantiation process of objects in order to make a system flexible with respect to object creation, object composition, and object representation. *Structural patterns* are used for composition of classes and objects to form larger structures by composition of interfaces and implementations. *Behavioral patterns* deal with algorithms and the assignment of responsibilities between objects.

Design Pattern versus Essential Construction Principles

Most of the design patterns of the catalog have a strong resemblance to one of the essential construction principles. Pree has shown that 14 of the 23 patterns in the GoF catalog can be derived from one of the essential construction principles introduced in section 1.1.1 [Pre95].

As an example, figure 1.6 on the next page depicts this relation for the Composite design pattern and the Composite construction principle. The pattern classes *Component*, Composite, and Leaf map to the corresponding construction principle classes *Composite_H*, Composite_T, and Composite_Leaf respectively. The composition relation children specified in the pattern maps to the children composition of the construction principle. In addition, the operations of the pattern classes map to the operations of the construction principle classes; *Component:: operation* maps to *Composite_H::template_hook*, Composite::operation maps to Composite_T:: template_hook, and Leaf::operation maps to Composite_Leaf::template_hook. These operation mappings are not shown in the figure 1.6.

Two design patterns are based on the Hook-Method principle, nine design patterns are based on the Hook-Object principle and three design patterns are essential construction principles themselves (Chain-Of-Responsibility, Decorator and Composite). The structure of the latter three design patterns, however, is more specific and more detailed compared to the corresponding construction principles. See, for instance, the Composite example in figure 1.6. Table 1.2 on the following page lists the relation between catalog design patterns and essential construction principles in detail.[5]

---

[5]Design patterns that are not relevant for the construction of frameworks are put into parentheses.

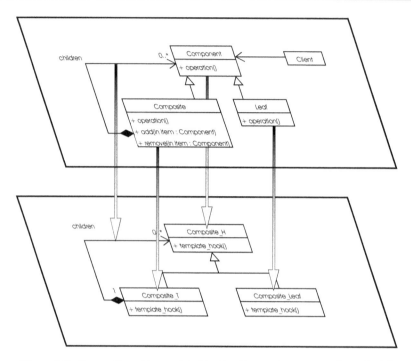

Figure 1.6: Composite pattern related to the Composite construction principle

Table 1.2: Design pattern based on construction principles

Category	GoF Pattern	Hook-M.	Hook-O.	Compos.	Decorator	COR
Creational	Abstract Factory		×			
Patterns	Builder		×			
	Factory Method	×				
	Prototype		×			
	(Singleton)					
Structural	Bridge		×			
Patterns	Composite			×		
	Decorator				×	
	(Adapter)					
Continued on next page ...						

Table 1.2: Design pattern based on construction principles

Category	GoF Pattern	Hook-M.	Hook-O.	Compos.	Decorator	COR
	(Facade)					
	(Flyweight)					
	(Proxy)					
Behavioral	Chain Of Resp.					×
Patterns	Command		×			
	Interpreter		×			
	Observer		×			
	Strategy		×			
	State		×			
	Template Method	×				
	(Iterator)					
	(Mediator)					
	(Memento)					
	(Visitor)					

Observer – A Design Pattern Example

One of the most prominent design patterns of the catalog is the *Observer* pattern, which presented as an example here. The purpose of the Observer pattern is to *"define a one-to-many dependency between objects so that when one object changes state, all its dependents are notified and updated automatically."* [GHJV95, p. 293]

The pattern is described as follows:

Pattern Name: Observer

Problem: When splitting a system into a set of cooperating classes, a common problem is to ensure the consistency of the related objects. Tight coupling is a possible but undesirable solution since it makes reuse more difficult.

An example of such a system is an application that separates user interface related components from the core application data. Changes in the application data have to be propagated to the user interface to ensure consistency. Moreover, several different view components might be used to represent the same data object. This implies that all views have to be updated whenever the corresponding data object's state changes.

Solution: Figure 1.7 on the next page shows the pattern's structure. The key classes are *Subject* and *Observer*. A subject might have associated an arbitrary number of observers, which subscribe themselves to the subject by using its attach method. On every event that changes the subject's internal state, it notifies its observers by sending them the *update* message. They are then responsible to gather the subject's state. In this solution, the subject state is accessible through the getState method which returns an instance of the state class SubjectState.

Consequences: The observer pattern allows for flexible and dynamic variation of observers and subjects. Since subjects are decoupled from concrete observers, they are potential candidates for reuse. In addition, new observers can be added to the system without affecting any of the existing subjects.

Another consequence of the application of this pattern is that broadcast communication is used to propagate the *update* message.

A drawback of this solution is that observers have no knowledge of each other. An observer performing a minor change on the subject's state may thus unintentionally cause a cascade of updates whose costs are not predictable by the updating observer.

In the presented solution the observers have to query the whole subject's state whenever they receive the update message. For large state objects, it can be expensive to visualize the whole state or to deduce what has changed since the last update. In such cases a more sophisticated update protocol might be required.

A comparison of the pattern structure in figure 1.7 on the facing page with the essential construction principle presented in the previous section shows that the Observer pattern is based on the *Hook-Object* principle, which is shown in figure 1.2 on page 7. *Subject* can be identified as template class, and the *Observer* defines the hook interface, which is implemented in ConctreteObserver. Template method and hook method can be identified as notify and *update*, respectively.

1.1.3   Architectural Patterns

A set of patterns concerned with the architecture of software systems is presented by Buschmann et al. [BMR+96]. An *architectural pattern*[6] is a basic structuring principle of software systems concerned with the assignment of responsibilities and relations to a set of predefined subsystems and their organization. Architectural patterns are defined on a higher level of abstraction than

---

[6]Originally, the term *architectural framework* was used [BMR+96]. To avoid confusion with the concept of object-oriented application frameworks, later the term *architectural pattern* was adopted [Vil01, p. 6].

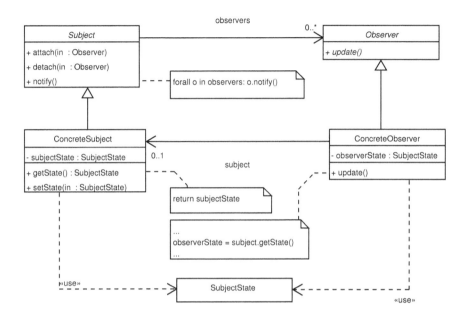

Figure 1.7: Observer structure

design patters, since they deal with subsystems instead of classes and objects. They provide support for the system architect to achieve certain system properties, for instance separation of the user interface from the core application functionality.

The authors use the following categorization to organize the pattern catalog:

From Mud to Structure: The purpose of patterns in this category is to decompose the overall system tasks into smaller, cooperating subtasks. To achieve that goal the system is split into parts that are described using a high level of abstraction.

An example for a decomposition is the construction of a system as a stack of layers.

Distributed Systems: In an environment where components are distributed over different computing entities, this kind of patterns is used to achieve proper system architectures.

The basic idea of *Broker* pattern, for example, is to decouple clients from servers by the introduction of a separate entity, the *broker*. The broker is responsible for their coordination and communication.

Interactive Systems: Patterns in this category deal with systems that have to provide a human-computer interface. They provide a system structure that separates the user interface from the application's core functionality.

The *Model-View-Controller* pattern, which is described in the next section, is a pattern of this category.

Adaptable Systems: High adaptability and extensibility, sometimes even at runtime, are common requirements for modern software systems. Patterns in this category provide appropriate system architectures.

An example is the *Microkernel* pattern, which suggests separating an application's minimal core from extended functionality and customized parts. Extensions can use the functionality provided by the core as base for their implementation.

Model-View-Controller – An Exemplary Architectural Pattern

The *Model-View-Controller* pattern splits an interactive application or subsystem into three distinct components with different responsibilities. Figure 1.8 on the facing page depicts the pattern's basic structure.

Model: This component represents the core application functionality, together with its data elements. Its responsibilities includes the encapsulation of application state (coreData), the processing of state queries (getData), the exposition of application functionality (service), and the notification of state changes (notify).

View: Views, the application's presentation components, are responsible for the visualization of the Model data. More than one view can display the same data element. Views request the required data from the Model directly and forward user inputs to a Controller component.

Controller: Controllers are responsible for processing user input, which means they map user actions to Model-updates, and they select the View responsible for the application's response. View and Controller components together represent the application's user interface.

To ensure consistency between user interface and model data, a notification mechanism is employed. This mechanism is an adapted version of the Observer pattern, discussed in section 1.1.2 on page 13. In the variant of the Model-View-Controller pattern presented here, both the abstract and the concrete subjects are incorporated into the Model class.

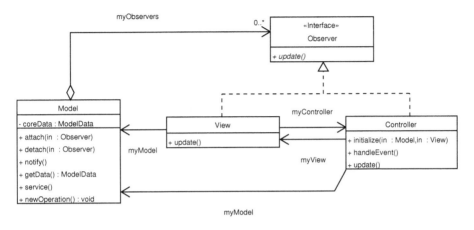

Figure 1.8: Model-View-Controller structure

Similarly to the identification of Observer pattern roles, template and hook roles can be identified for the Model-View-Controller pattern. The Model can be identified as template for extending the system with new user interface components, whereas View and Controller are the hooks for that purpose. Such a mapping, however, can not be identified for all patterns of the catalog, since most of the architectural patterns are represented on a higher level of abstraction. For instance, patterns describing subsystems only do not allow to identify templates and hooks on class or on method level.

1.1.4   Discussion on Patterns

The patterns and catalogs presented here are prominent examples of a variety of approaches. The appearance of the GoF pattern catalog [GHJV95] inspired many authors working in different application domains to provide their expert knowledge in form of patterns. For instance, there are pattern catalogs for business modeling and for software testing. Coad describes a so-called *Domain Neutral Component* that can be used in any business domain as basis for class modeling, in the analysis phase, and also in the design phase [CLD99]. Patterns of that type, which describe how to come to a solution rather than to give one particular solution, are also known as *generative patterns* [Mat96]. Bad design practices and choices leading to problems in later development stages sometimes also are presented in a form similar to design patterns; they are called *Anti-Patterns*.

The growth of published patterns makes it hard to organize patterns. But to be able to efficiently find an appropriate pattern for a particular problem, it is essential to have the set of available patterns organized reasonably. If the set gets too big, for instance by many patterns for similar problems with just slightly different solutions, the effort required to evaluate possible patterns increases. Consequently, either the time benefit promised by the pattern approach shrinks, or the quality of the pattern selection decreases.

Patterns allow software designers to build flexible solutions. Excessive use of patterns, however, can lead to systems that are *too* flexible. In other words, the amount of complexity introduced by the additional flexibility is inappropriate when compared to the problem's complexity itself. This also is the case when the evaluation of pattern alternatives for a certain problem is not done properly; often the most flexible pattern instead of the most appropriate pattern is chosen. Such bad decisions usually are made by novice and inexperienced pattern users.

Essential construction principles only capture the structural aspects of a software design [Vil01]. They denote the classification of the roles classes or methods play in relation to each other. Since design patterns usually provide different implementation alternatives, essential construction principles can be used to explicitly document the design decisions when applying a certain pattern variation.

1.2   Frameworks – Architectural Reuse

The decomposition of large software systems into separate modules requires a proper, preliminary definition of interfaces between these modules [Par72]. Decomposition and interface definitions also are useful for the production families of programs [Par76]: when producing program families, it is worthwhile to study the common properties of the family members first, and then determine the special properties of each family member. In a module-based approach, first the module interfaces are specified and default implementations are provided. Then the default implementation is substituted by an implementation specific to the family member to be built. A family member does not have to use all modules available for the family, using just subsets is possible. For instance, in a family of operating systems, some installations might require just a subset of the available system functions and thus may not include certain modules such as the printing module.

Early approaches on reuse of common components[7] in a family of programs focused on the identification of common functionality and how to encapsulate them into reusable modules. The emergence of the object-technology paradigm influenced the construction of program families.

---

[7]Fontoura et al. define a *component* as a *"piece of software with a programming interface, deployable as unit"* [FPR01, p. 5].

With the appearance of *object-oriented application frameworks*, the focus shifted from reusable modules towards reusable software architectures.

The term *Framework (FW)* is, according to Bosch and Van Gurp, defined as *"a partial design and implementation for an application in a given domain"* [BV01, p. 277]. This definition implies that a framework is an incomplete system. The task of completing the missing parts by providing a particular implementation is called *framework instantiation* or *framework adaptation* [Vil01]. A definition of object-oriented frameworks that incorporates the most prominent definitions proposed in literature is given by Mattsson: *"A (generative) architecture designed for maximum reuse, represented as a collective set of abstract and concrete classes; encapsulated potential behavior for subclassed specializations"* [Mat96, p. 52]. Fontoura et al. remark that frameworks are *"semi-finished pieces of software"* that are extensible through the *"callback-style of programming"* [FPR02, p. 188].

1.2.1   Characterization of Frameworks

For wide variety of application domains frameworks have been built: user interface frameworks, hypermedia systems [Vil01], distributed systems [FJ00, part III], computer-integrated manufacturing [FJ00, part I], supercomputing [FJ00, chapter 14], embedded systems [FJ00, chapter 16], networking and telecommunications [FJ00, part 5], satellite control systems [PP00], VLSI routing algorithms [Vil01], local search heuristics [FLA+01], and many more.

Bosch and Van Gurp propose to use the targeted problem domain as criterion to group frameworks into three different categories [BV01]:

Application frameworks: Frameworks in this category provide a full range of functionality that typically is needed by an application program. This may include user interface, database, persistence, security, and so on.

Domain frameworks: Domain frameworks provide support for the implementation of software systems targeted to a certain application domain. Examples of application domains are banking systems, payroll systems, enterprise portals, and alarm systems. Since domain specific software usually has to be tailored to a customer's specific needs or has to be developed from scratch, frameworks offer a great potential to reduce development time as well as product costs.

Support frameworks: Support frameworks usually address very specific domains closely related to software systems such as installation, error logging, threading, and memory management. Support frameworks mostly are used in combination with domain or application frameworks and ease the development work by providing comfortable interfaces for certain program aspects.

White-Box versus Black-Box Reuse

An important aspect for characterizing frameworks is the adaptation mechanism they enforce [BV01, FPR01, Vil01].

White-box reuse employs inheritance and dynamic binding: framework application classes inherit from (abstract) framework classes and predefined hook methods [8] are overridden. This implies that the adaptation process's success relies on the developer's framework knowledge, which can be gained by reading framework documentation, by attending training, or by reviewing template implementations.

Black-box reuse, in contrast, only relies on the specification of components and their interfaces. Black-box framework adaptation is performed by combining concrete framework classes, already shipped with the framework as components, using object composition and delegation.

Pure black-box reuse limits the flexibility of a framework since applications can only use the provided component implementations. Frameworks therefore usually utilize both mechanisms, which can be achieved through a multi-layer design. A white-box layer that defines the framework architecture consists of interfaces and abstract classes. The black-box layer uses the white-box layer via inheritance and provides concrete classes and components that are ready use; they can be plugged into the architecture to build an application by black-box reuse. In situations where the predefined black-box components do not provide enough flexibility, a customized component can be implemented in white-box manner. Section 1.2.2 provides a detailed discussion of that approach.

Control Flow

The core characteristic of a framework is that it abides by the *Hollywood Principle*: *"Don't call us, we'll call you!"* This principle is also known as the *Greyhound Principle – "Leave the driving to us!"* [App98]. Basically, this means that the framework is responsible for calling framework adaptation code that is plugged into a hot spot; the call sequence follows a predefined interaction protocol. This so-called *inverted flow of control* differentiates frameworks from traditional programming libraries.

---

[8]*Hooks* in the context of frameworks are also called *hot spots* or *variation points* [Pre95].

In most cases, the framework contains the main event loop, and it is responsible for calling the application specific methods in response to occurring events. In other words, the control flow is managed by the framework. Frameworks of that type are called *calling frameworks* [Vil01]. Application and domain frameworks typically control the main flow of events.

Called frameworks, also referred to as *invoked frameworks*, do not contain the main event loop and are called by the application in response to external events. Support frameworks usually are implemented as called frameworks.

Framelets

Developing frameworks is expensive and difficult, and using frameworks is not trivial either; a lot of issues have to be considered. For example, the training phase for large frameworks potentially is very expensive. Combining several large frameworks in one application also can be very complicated, which will be addressed in more detail in the next section. To avoid these issues, Pree and Koskimies propose the usage of small, flexible, and reusable assets called *Framelets* [PK99]. Such *mini-frameworks* are special regarding to the following properties:

Size: Framelets are *small* compared to traditional frameworks. Typically, they consist of fewer than ten classes.

Control Flow: They are *invoked frameworks*, i.e. they do not assume the main control of the application. Nevertheless, they also follow the Hollywood principle such that adaptation code is called following a certain interaction protocol.

Interface: Framelets have a *clearly defined and simple interface*. More precisely, framelets have two interfaces: one interface for calling the framelet in order to request its service, and a second interface that can be used for adaptation.

1.2.2   Development and Evolution of Frameworks

A framework is said to be *well-designed* if it provides adequate *hot spots* required for adaptation [Pre99]. Hot spots can be components designed for composition, i.e. for black-box reuse, or as abstract methods for adaptation by inheritance, i.e. for white-box reuse. Furthermore, mature framework architectures ideally introduce a clear separation between black-box and white-box artifacts [Vil01].

Figure 1.9 on the following page shows a simplified structure of a typical framework design. Note that this figure is a slightly modified version of the structure described by Viljamaa [Vil01].

This layered structure separates three different concerns of a framework architecture:

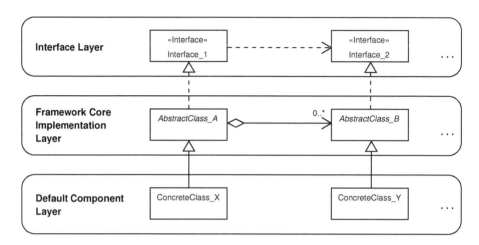

Figure 1.9: Schematic structure of a typical framework

Interface layer: Interfaces build the top layer. They specify the framework's basic concepts, their relationships, and the services they provide.

Framework core implementation layer: Abstract classes that implement the interfaces form the middle layer. These classes define the default framework behavior. It is intended that this implementation is used in most framework instances without modification. The abstract classes can define abstract methods that have to be overridden during framework instantiation in case a white-box adaptation is necessary.

Default component layer: The bottom layer contains default implementations for commonly required adaptations of the core implementation layer. These components serve as black-box hot spots as well as reference code for white-box adaptations.

In a real framework, the layers typically are not as clearly separated as it is sketched in figure 1.9. Since no framework is ideal from its beginning [Pre99], the initial design usually is reviewed several times and altered in certain aspects. As a result, the layer borders might become blurred over time.

Framework development is not a straight development process; framework development is a highly iterative activity. The term *framework development* thus stands for both, the initial design and the framework's evolution [Pre99]. In addition, a framework cannot be assumed to be stable after its first release. The layers of a mature framework are relatively stable. Nevertheless, ongoing changes of requirements demand for changes in the software, so also frameworks evolve over time. Viljamaa describes the evolution process as a bottom-up activity [Vil01]: As the framework is instantiated several times, a number of similar white-box adaptations are developed. Parts of their common behavior is generalized and added to the default component layer. New functional requirements are then discovered in the default component layer. Consequently, the higher layers, i.e. the framework core implementation layer and the interface layer, are subject to further change activities.

One key problem in framework development is to find appropriate domain abstractions. For this task, which mostly takes place in the early development stages, in-depth domain knowledge is necessary [FPR01, chapter 7], [FSJ99b]. In addition, it is critical for the success of the framework that its design is as flexible as necessary, but also as easy to use as possible. Extreme flexibility often introduces an unnecessary dimension of complexity, resulting in a framework that is difficult to understand and awkward to use. Frequently, this problem is introduced by excessive use of inadequate design patterns, as described in section 1.1.4.

A framework, however, can not be changed to any extend. Because a framework's interfaces are published, there might be running systems that depend on them. So framework changes often have to be compatible with existing systems.

Development Roles

Four user roles can be identified during the whole life cycle of a framework [PRST99]: The *framework developer* builds the core framework. Components based on a framework are built by the *component developer* and integrated in the original framework. These components are assembled into a custom application by the *application developer*. This application is used by the *end user*.

More than one role can be taken by the same person, and a person can change roles: A framework developer might be responsible for providing components, a component developer might develop application programs, and an end user might build custom applications.

1.2.3 Documentation of Frameworks

An application developer cannot use a framework without a basic understanding of the interactions and functionality essential to the framework design [PP01]. For a successful adaptation of a framework, it is essential to communicate the basic principles used for the design to the framework users. In particular, the locations of hot spots and how they are instantiated is important information, and these aspects have to be documented thoroughly [Vil01]. Since the classes in a framework are designed to work together, framework users have to learn the basics of most of the classes in order to be able to understand their interaction patterns.

When learning the usage of a framework, examples play an important role. Whether they are code samples or predefined black-box components, examining how an existing adaptation works helps to quickly find the variation points needed to achieve a certain behavior. Usually, several examples have to be studied to understand different usages of a single hot spot. Providing compact, yet comprehensive examples, however, is a difficulty of its own [Vil01].

Documentation Audience Roles

In order to provide appropriate documentation that efficiently communicates essential information, it is necessary to identify the potential audience of a framework's documentation. Mattsson describes the following audiences [Mat96] [9]:

Decision makers: A decision maker has to decide which framework is used in a particular application software project. The documentation needed should describe the framework's capabilities, its basic features, and also the consequences introduced by a framework. Brief examples are recommended.

There is no equivalent development role for this audience among the roles described in section 1.2.2.

Framework users: Framework users are software engineers that use the framework in the way it is intended by the framework developers. The documentation targeted for this audience has to describe the basic framework concepts, list the variation points, and has to give detailed instructions on how these variation points are adapted. Examples are integral parts of the documentation for framework users.

The *application developer role* and the *component developer role* discussed in section 1.2.2 correspond to the audience *framework users*.

Framework experts: This audience is the usually small group of developers that actually modifies or extends the framework itself. An in-depth understanding of the framework architecture, the abstractions and algorithms used, the interactions of the framework components, and the ramifications of possible changes is necessary. The documentation should comprehensively describe all these topics.

The *framework experts audience* mainly consists of *framework developers*, but also *component developers* might be interested in the documentation for framework experts to get

---

[9]Mattsson originally did not assign names to the audience groups [Mat96]. Here the names are introduced to be able to unambiguously refer to them in later chapters.

a better understanding of the framework internals, which might be necessary for certain white-box adaptations.

Documentation Techniques

Due to the importance of appropriate framework documentation, several approaches have been proposed to improve the quality of these documents:

General modeling techniques: They support the architectural description of software systems in general. This might be a standardized modeling language such as the *Unified Modeling Language* [Bur99, JRH+03], or a multi-perspective approach, such as the *4+1 View Model* [Kru95]. Neither of these approaches has explicit support for frameworks. Extensions to these modeling techniques specific to frameworks also have been proposed. *UML-F* [FPR01] is such an extension for the UML and is discussed in chapter 2.

Framework cookbooks: Cookbooks are informal or semiformal descriptions on how the framework has to be used. Cookbooks can guide the application developer during framework instantiation in a step-by-step manner. They consist of several *recipes* that describe how to add functionality to the application, or how to solve particular problems, by using the framework [Vil01].

Fontoura and Pree describe a cookbook approach based on UML-F [FPR01, chapter 5].

Object-oriented patterns: Patterns are well suited for the documentation of frameworks since they give explicit information about the decisions that have been made in the framework's design. Moreover, most patterns described in the catalogs of Gamma et al. [GHJV95] and Buschmann et al. [BMR+96] are closely related to frameworks, since they were discovered by examining a number of frameworks [Vil01]. Using patterns for describing framework architectures helps framework users to see their adaptations in a perspective on a higher level of abstraction than that of single classes.

A problem with patterns is that one class can play different roles in more than one pattern; drawing sharp borderlines between patterns therefore is not always possible [Don02, Mat96, FPR01].

Framework description languages: Another approach to document a framework is to use a formal language. Inheritance relationships, references and object creation sequences are the essential building block of such a description [Mat96]. In addition, information for the adaptation process also has to be included. These are, for instance, composition rules, subclassing constraints, and infrastructure requirements.

Fayad et al. mention that the cost of providing suitable framework documentation is very high and that keeping the documentation up-to-date is a difficult problem of its own [FSJ99a]. Nevertheless, appropriate framework documentation that suits the needs of all possible audiences is one of the key elements for the success of a framework. Even a well-designed framework that provides outstanding features cannot overcome the effort needed to learn its usage; inadequate documentation therefore is at least as bad as lack in usability.

1.2.4   Framework Adaptation

"Reusing a framework is hard" [PK00, p. 57]. A framework consists of the core classes of an application, thus the application developer has to understand its basic architecture to be able to adapt the framework. Usually the first instantiation of a framework is the most difficult one. For that reason it is advisable to do it under the guidance of an expert [FSJ99a]. Building an application by using a framework can require one or more of the following activities [BV01]:

Writing glue code: When the components provided by the framework cover all requirements they have to meet, they just have to be configured and glued together in a black-box fashion to form the application. This can be done either by writing the glue code by hand, or the glue code can be generated by a tool. Speaking in terms of developer roles defined in section 1.2.2, the *application developer* is responsible for this activity.

In the ideal case, that is when the framework components cover the whole set of application requirements, this is the only activity needed.

Providing application specific components: If the application requirements do not match the features provided by the framework components exactly, it is necessary to create application specific components. The *component developer* is the role associated with this activity.

Since these application specific adaptations are encapsulated in components, they are potential candidates for being reused in similar applications. Later on, these components might be added to the framework's default component layer.

Providing application specific classes: If the required functionality is outside the scope of the framework, application specific classes have to be created. It is the *application developer's* job to write these classes.

Reuse potential for this kind of adaptation in the first place exists only through plain code reuse. If the required functionality is needed more often, it may be worthwhile to build a new framework, or framelet, or even to extend the existing framework.

A problematic situation arises if more than one framework is used to build an application; in particular if they are *calling frameworks*, that is, they assume control over the application's main flow of events. Garlan, Allen and Ockerbloom describe a real-world project that struggled with this kind of problems [GAO95].

Tool support for framework adaptation has been proposed by several researchers. Active approaches such as active cookbooks [PPSS95] and dynamic task lists [Vil01] actively guide through the adaptation process. Adaptation cases [FPR01, chapter 7] define the mapping between requirements and adaptations needed, which are stated as cookbook recipes. Adaptation reports describe problem situations that occurred in concrete framework instantiation projects.

CHAPTER 2

A UML Extension for Object-Oriented Framework Architectures

The *Unified Modeling Language (UML)* is a general purpose visual modeling language. It is emerging as the standard notation for the diagrammatic description of complex software systems. UML diagrams are widely used to specify, to model, to document, and to visualize a software system at various levels of abstraction. Notational elements for describing static and dynamic aspects of a software system are defined in the language's specification documents. Systems described by UML models typically are based on the object-oriented paradigm.

Object-oriented frameworks offer a huge potential for improving productivity of software development through reuse in the large scale – they provide the potential of reusing architectural designs [PK00]. Due to their complexity and size, however, they are hard to develop and also hard to reuse. Both activities require a good understanding of the framework architecture, thus demanding for a well-suited design notation. As a consequence, the number of frameworks designed using UML is continuously increasing, and framework vendors often provide parts of the product documentation in form of UML diagrams.

The Unified Modeling Language, a large and complex language whose current version is *UML 2*, is neither complete nor absolutely consistent [JRH+03, CKW+99]. As a general purpose OO modeling language, it is not well suited for all application domains, since certain application domains have very special requirements on a modeling language. To overcome that problem, the UML defines extension mechanisms, such as the *UML Profile* mechanism, that allows for customization of the basic language.

The *UML-F profile* is an extension to the Unified Modeling Language that aims at the framework domain: Through explicit annotation of design patterns and template-hook roles, it is made easier for both, the developer creating or maintaining the framework, and the developer building applications using a framework, to understand the framework architecture and to be able to detect variation points and their instantiation requirements quickly.

This chapter first gives a short introduction to UML and the profile extension mechanism. Second, the basic concepts of the UML-F language extensions are explained and some specifics of profile mechanisms are described to the necessary detail. The description of UML-F is mostly based on the book of Fontoura, Pree and Rumpe [FPR01], but also other publications by the same authors have been used as reference [FPR00, FPR02]. Due to the fact that the profile mechanism has changed from prior versions to UML 2, a new structure for the UML-F profile is presented here, which is compatible to the UML 2 profile mechanism.

2.1 The Unified Modeling Language

The *Unified Modeling Language* is a standard modeling language targeted at object oriented software systems [CKW+99]. The UML defines a graphical notation used to describe a system from different perspectives at different levels of abstraction.

The current language version, *UML 2.0*, has passed the standardization process of the *Object Management Group (OMG)* [JRH+03], and is the successor of the widely used version 1.5 [OMG03c]. In this chapter the UML version 2.0 is discussed. If the provided information is related to an older language version, it is explicitly stated.

Diagrams

Diagrams are used to describe the model elements and their relationships. Modeling different system views is achieved by using different diagram types. These are defined in the UML standard and point out certain aspects of a system using various levels of abstraction. The diagram types can be categorized into two groups [JRH+03]:

Structure diagrams are used to describe model elements that are irrespective of time. The most important structure diagram type is the *class diagram*, which is used to describe the static structure of the system. It contains significant structure relations and data types. *Object diagrams* are closely related to class diagrams; system snapshots at certain points in time are shown at the same hierarchical level as shown in the class diagram. Object diagrams are well suited to visualize cardinalities and object proportions. Other structure diagram types are the *package diagram*, which models the organization of the system model into larger units called *packages*, the *composite structure diagram*, which is used for top-down modeling of whole-part hierarchies, the *component diagram*, which shows the organization and dependencies of technical system components, and the *deployment diagram*, which models the runtime environment at a very high level of abstraction.

Behavior diagrams   describe behavioral features, that is, the dynamic properties of model elements. *Use case diagrams* use a high level of abstraction to present the outside view of the system; it specifies the basic features the system provides to its environment. *Activity diagrams* describe the execution of a flow-oriented process in detail by using conditions, loops, and branches. Parallelism and synchronization can also be modeled. *State machine diagrams* are used for precise specifications of state models.

Interaction diagrams form a subdivision of behavior diagrams that emphasize on interaction aspects between objects. The most important member of this group is the *sequence diagram*. Its intended use is to describe the information interchange between communication partners by precisely specifying the possible message sequences. Modeling parallelism and control flow, i.e. conditions, loops, and branches, is supported.

Communication diagrams give an overview of information interchange between system components. They are, however, not very detailed. *Timing diagrams*, in contrast, precisely specify the behavior of model elements in the temporal domain.

Interaction overview diagrams link interaction diagrams at the top-level by using a high level of abstraction.

Language Extensions

The Unified Modeling Language is extensible by design. Certain application domains require specific modeling elements so that a modeling language can be used efficiently. The UML defines extension mechanisms that allow customizing the language. For that reason, it actually can be regarded as a family of languages [CKW+99].

Two basic extension mechanisms are defined in the UML standard:

Heavyweight extensions   are based on the definition of a new language as an alternative to the UML. The mechanism provided by OMG for defining modeling languages is used for that purpose [FFVM04]. The syntax and semantics of new language elements are defined such that they exactly fit the specific domain requirements. This approach results in very specific modeling languages that may use parts of the UML, but they are by no means compatible to the UML. Existing CASE tools that support the UML therefore cannot be used for the new language without customization. So-called *meta-modeling tools* provide functionality for defining modeling languages.

UML profiles are specializations of the Unified Modeling Language, also referred to as *lightweight* extensions. Profiles are fully compatible with UML since they respect the UML metamodel and do not change the semantics of UML elements. They specialize some language elements and impose new restrictions on them. Section 2.1.2 discusses this extension mechanism in detail.

2.1.1   UML Language Architecture

The UML is designed as a layered architecture, which allows defining the UML in UML terminology itself. In other words, the modeling language UML is defined in terms of a modeling language that uses the same language constructs. Since UML is used to define models, i.e. the user-models, it represents a *meta-model*. Consequently, the model UML is based on is a *meta-metamodel*. Taking also the system built using the user-model, i.e. the target system, into account, one can identify four model layers. This UML layer system is called the *four-layer metamodel hierarchy*.

Figure 2.1 on the facing page shows the language layers and the relations between them schematically (adapted from [KHB03] and [OMG03e]). On the left side the model layers are represented as packages together with the layer name. The right side shows examples for every layer.

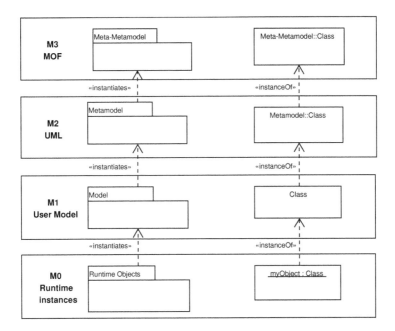

Figure 2.1: Four-layer metamodel hierarchy

M3: This basic architecture layer builds the foundation for building metamodels. It is called the *meta-metamodel* layer and is the model for layer *M2* elements.

The language used for describing *M3* layer elements is called *Meta Object Facility (MOF)* and is also standardized by the Object Management Group. MOF is a language to describe metamodels and it is used to define modeling languages like UML or even MOF itself [FFVM04].

M2: Layer *M2*, the *metamodel* layer, is the layer the UML resides on. *M2* layer elements are models for the elements in layer *M1*. The concepts defined on this layer, e.g. *Class*, *Association*, and *Attribute*, are used to model elements of layer *M1*. *M2* model elements are instances of *M3* model elements.

M1: The user-model layer contains the model of the target system. Elements of layer *M1* are *models*. Examples of model elements at this layer are concepts like *Person, Car* or *Garage*.

A user model element is an instance of a UML metamodel element. It may contain both, model elements and snapshots of instances of these model elements [OMG03e]. The snapshots are constrained versions of the corresponding instances at level *M0*.

M0: This layer represents the running system. It contains run-time instances of the model elements defined at layer *M1*.

The UML standard uses the four-layer metamodel hierarchy to organize the standard documents. The document called *UML Infrastructure* describes the meta-metamodel [OMG03e]. This document also is the basis for the second version of MOF, OMG's meta-metamodel language [KHB03]. Another separate document defines the UML itself: The so-called *UML Superstructure* uses the concepts defined in the UML Infrastructure to express the syntax and semantics of the UML 2 elements [OMG03d]. Since it is not possible to express the complete semantics of all UML 2 elements by using just UML Infrastructure vocabulary, additional *constraints* are used. A constraint is a Boolean expression that is bound to a certain context [KHB03]. Constraints are stated in the *Object Constraint Language (OCL)*, which is standardized by the OMG, too [OMG03b].

2.1.2   UML Profiles

Extending the UML using the lightweight *profile* mechanism is achieved by UML specialization. Some of the language elements are specialized and new restrictions are imposed on them, while the UML metamodel is respected and the original semantics of the UML elements are unchanged [FFVM04]. The profile mechanism is not a first-class extension mechanism. In other words, existing metamodels cannot be modified and it is not allowed to remove existing constraints that apply to the metamodel. Thus, the extension is strictly additive to the standard UML semantics.

A UML profile is *"a stereotyped package that contains model elements that have been customized for a specific domain or purpose using extension mechanisms, such as stereotypes, tagged definitions and constraints. A profile may also specify model libraries on which it depends and the metamodel subset that it extends"* [OMG03d, p. 13].

This means that a UML profile is a UML package stereotyped «*profile*»[1]. It can extend either a metamodel or another profile [FFVM04]. Profiles thus can form hierarchies, where profiles at the bottom of the extension hierarchy are the most specialized ones, and the UML standard is at the hierarchy's top.

---

[1] When a stereotype is applied to a model element, the name of the stereotype is shown within a pair of guillemets « ». If more than one stereotype is applied to a model element, the stereotype names are shown as a comma separated list within the guillemets.

Profiles are defined in terms of three basic mechanisms [OMG03e]:

Stereotypes: A stereotype is a class that defines how an existing *Metaclass* or stereotype may be extended. It enables the use of platform or domain specific terminology or notation, which can be used additionally to stereotypes already defined for the extended metaclass. Stereotypes are defined as classes stereotyped «*stereotype*». A stereotype metaclass is associated to the metamodel elements that correspond to the model elements that should be extensible by the stereotype.

Stereotypes typically are used to classify model elements for the purpose of imposing additional properties or restrictions on them.

The UML Superstructure already predefines a set of stereotypes [OMG03d, appendix B]. The stereotype is the primary extension construct of a profile. The stereotype metamodel element is specified in the UML Infrastructure [OMG03e, chapter 13.1.7].

Tagged Values: The explicit definition of a property as a name-value pair is called a tagged value. Its name is called the tag. Tagged values are modeled as meta-attributes of a stereotype metaclass. Certain tags are predefined by the UML.

Constraints: Constraints are semantic conditions or restrictions. Constraints usually are stated in *OCL* [OMG03b], but they can be stated in any language, for instance in natural language text or in a formal mathematical notation. When attached to a stereotype metaclass, constraints impose restrictions on the model elements extended by that stereotype.

Technically spoken, the UML package Core::Profile contains the mechanisms that allow for the extension of metaclasses to adapt them for domain specific purposes [OMG03e]. Thus, the profile mechanism resides in the M2 layer only. In contrast, the heavyweight extension mechanism also uses layer M3 to define new layer M2 elements.

A UML Profile Example for Network Models

To illustrate how the concepts described in the previous section are applied, a simple profile Network for network models is used as an example. The profile definition is shown in figure 2.2 on the next page.

On the left side the two metaclasses Class and AssociationClass represent the UML metamodel elements that are to be extended. The stereotypes are specified by the stereotype metaclasses NeworkNode, RoutingNode and NetworkConnection. A RoutingNode is a specialization of a

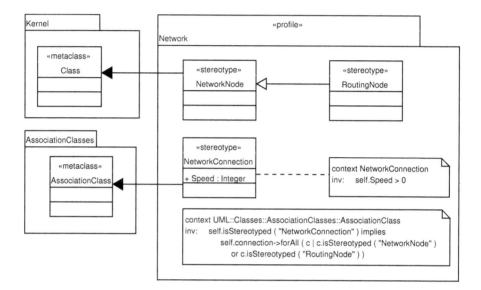

Figure 2.2: UML profile for network models

NetworkNode. The two extension associations[2] define that the stereotypes «*networknode*» and
«*routingnode*» can be added to classes, whereas association classes can be stereotyped as «*networkconnection*». The tagged value Speed is defined for the latter stereotype. The two OCL
constraints given ensure that the network models built using this profile are consistent. The
first constraint restricts the values for the Speed-tag to be positive only. The second constraint
is a bit more involved. Its purpose is to ensure that association classes that are stereotyped
«*networkconnection*» may connect classes that are stereotyped «*networknode*» or «*routingnode*» only.

If a model package wants to use a certain UML profile, it has to *apply*[3] the profile. Figure 2.3
on the facing page depicts the graphical notation used for that purpose: A model package called
RouterModel applies the Network profile.

Figure 2.4 on the next page shows a class diagram that contains the model elements defined in

_____

[2]The *Extension* is a metamodel element newly introduced in UML 2. It is a kind of association and used
to indicate that the properties of a metaclass are extended through a stereotype. *Extensions* give the ability
to flexibly add stereotypes to classes and later remove them from classes. The notation for an *Extension* is
an arrow pointing from a stereotype to the extended class, where the arrowhead is shown as a filled triangle
[OMG03e, chapter 13.1.1].

[3]*ProfileApplication*, a metamodel element introduced in version 2 of the UML, is a kind of *PackageImport*
that adds the capability to state that a profile is applied to a package [OMG03e, chapter 13.1.6].

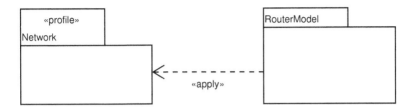

Figure 2.3: Application of the network profile

the package RouterModel. It models the routing aspect of a heterogeneous network, where two different network topologies are connected through a router. The router is depicted by the class Router; it has got the «*routingnode*» stereotype. The router's left hand side represents a star topology, whereas the right hand side of the router represents a line topology. Notes attached to the association classes stereotyped «*networkconnection*» assign values to the Speed-tags, as defined in the corresponding stereotype metaclass in diagram 2.2.

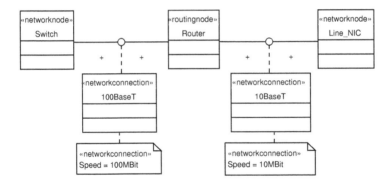

Figure 2.4: Network model using the network profile

2.2   The UML Profile for Framework Architectures

The intention of the *UML Profile for Framework Architectures (UML-F)* is to define subset of UML, enriched with UML-compliant extensions, that allows for the annotation of design patterns that are used to develop object-oriented framework architectures. The goals pursued by the UML-F profile are manifold:

Pattern annotation: The notational elements defined in UML-F allow for the precise annotation and thus documentation of design patterns used for the framework design.

Straightforward extensibility: UML-F itself uses the spirit of frameworks. It provides the basic mechanisms for formation of hierarchies of notational elements to describe design patterns. In addition, custom design patterns may be defined, which enables the profile to be customized for domain specific requirements.

Small set of notational elements: UML-F comprises a rather small set of mnemonic notational elements. This helps to keep the learning curve flat.

UML compliance: Since UML-F uses the lightweight profile extension mechanism defined by the UML standard, it is compatible with UML extensions provided by third parties – they may be used together at the same time. Another advantage of being compliant with the UML standard is that it eases the integration in off-the-shelf CASE tools.

Tool support: The notational elements defined in the UML-F profile are adequate for integration in UML CASE tools.

UML-F does not discuss all diagrams available in UML. Only diagrams essential to framework development, in particular class diagrams, object diagrams, and sequence diagrams, are considered. Other diagram types still are available, but since they play a minor role for framework development and framework adaptation, they are not covered by the profile [FPR01, chapter 2].

2.2.1   The Pattern Annotation Rationale

Using design patterns for the documentation of framework architectures usually is a good choice. By their very nature, they highlight variation points and roles that framework classes play. They also provide background information about the design decisions that drove the framework development. Frameworks often consist of *micro architectures* that can be considered as instances of design patterns.

Two shortcomings of design patterns make it necessary to complement this technique to be able to produce appropriate framework documentation. First, the granularity of design patterns is sometimes too coarse to be able to describe the design of a particular framework part. Second, design patterns do not always state the extension points clearly.

Using essential construction principles can prevent both problems, since they describe the fundamental mechanisms for adaptable object-oriented software at the finest granularity. This makes them the best choice to describe framework variation points. Furthermore, all design patterns that are relevant for framework design can be mapped to the essential construction principles that form their basis, as discussed in section 1.1.2, and in particular in table 1.2 on page 12. Thus, design patterns are complemented perfectly by essential construction principles for framework documentation purposes.

Frameworks are domain specific pieces of semi-finished software. Requirements specific to the application domain can not always be captured by general purpose design patterns. For that reason, domain specific design patterns often are used for the construction of a framework or a part of it. Domain specific patterns may be of arbitrary granularity: they may be at the same granularity level as the GoF patterns, they may use one or more of the catalog patterns as building blocks, or they may be even more specialized by expressing the solution structure in terms of other domain specific patterns. A comprehensive framework documentation approach should be able to document framework design decisions by using the domain specific patterns that drove the architecture design.

2.2.2   UML 1.3 Profile to UML 2.0 Profile Mapping

Originally, the UML-F profile was published using UML 1.3 [OMG99] as its base language [FPR01]. That UML version had not such a mature stereotype system as UML 2.0 has got. For example, model elements were limited to have at most one stereotype only. UML 1.3 also did not have a formally defined profile mechanism. Another problem was the ambiguity between stereotypes and tagged values: both mechanisms, although defined as strictly separate concepts, could be used for similar purposes.

For that reasons the notation of *UML-F tags* was introduced, which defines that stereotypes are treated as *synonyms* for tagged values.

The UML 2.0 precisely defines the semantics of profiles, stereotypes and tags. The profile presented here follows the UML 2.0 semantics. It was designed such that the tag definitions given in the original UML-F profile [FPR01] can be mapped to the new concepts easily:

- *UML-F tags* are defined as stereotypes.

- For tags of *Boolean* type, the appearance of the corresponding UML 2 stereotype equals to the value true. Consequently, the absence of the stereotype equals to the value false.

- For non-*Boolean* tags, the corresponding stereotype metaclass in the UML 2 profile is given a tag definition, i.e. a property, that can hold the tag value.

With this mapping it is easy to see that for the definition of new tags a tabular form, similar
to the tables used in the original profile [FPR01, chapter 3.6], can be used.

2.2.3   UML-F Profile for UML 2 Structure

As depicted in figure 2.5, the *UML-F profile*[4] is split into two separate profiles:

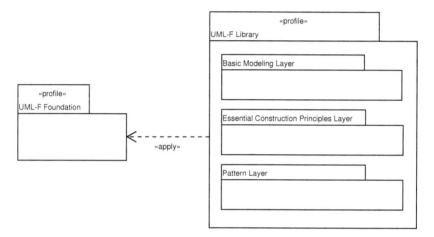

Figure 2.5: *UML-F profile* structure

The UML-F Foundation profile contains the conceptual framework that can be used to
define UML-F tags. It does not define any tags itself, but rather provides constructs and
base classes to be used in every other profile that defines UML-F tags.

The UML-F Library profile contains all basic UML-F tags. It does so by applying the
UML-F Foundation profile and by using the concepts defined there. The library profile is
structured in three layers, because construction principles, design patterns, and domain
specific patterns form a hierarchy of framework building blocks. Thus a layering approach
is used to organize UML-F tags into separate categories.

The UML-F profile's two-piece structure is the key to its extensibility. Domain specific patterns
can be defined by simply creating a separate profile package that applies the *UML-F Foundation*

---

[4]In this and all subsequent sections, the term *UML-F profile* is used synonymously to the full name "*UML-F
profile for UML 2*".

profile and by defining the corresponding UML-F tags. If they rely on design patterns or construction principles, also the *UML-F Library profile* is applied. Thus, UML-F pattern profiles form hierarchies of profiles. This makes it easy to reuse (domain specific) pattern definitions.

2.2.4 The UML-F Foundation Profile

Figure 2.6 shows the structure of the *UML-F Foundation profile*.

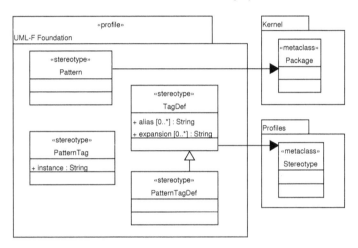

Figure 2.6: *UML-F Foundation profile* structure

The profile's elements are described as follows:

TagDef: This stereotype serves as marker for the definition of UML-F tags. Any stereotype that defines a UML-F tag has to be stereotyped «*TagDef*», or by any derived stereotype, such as «*PatternTagDef*». Two tagged values are defined as property of this stereotype:

        alias: A UML-F tag might have several names. The main name is defined as the stereotype's name. Alias names can be defined using this tagged value.

        expansion: A UML-F tag might be the specialization of one or more other UML-F tags. Speaking in UML-F terminology, a tag might *expand to* one or more other tags. This tagged value models the expansion relation by keeping the names of all UML-F tags the defined tag expands to.

PatternTagDef: UML-F tags that are part of a certain pattern are defined using the «*PatternTagDef*» stereotype. When a *pattern tag* is defined, the corresponding stereotype metaclass has to be a subclass of PatternTag.

PatternTag: This metaclass serves a base class for all UML-F pattern tag definitions. It defines the following tagged value:

        instance: Since a model element may play certain roles in more than one pattern, this tagged value can be used to specify the name of the corresponding pattern instance.

Pattern: This stereotype is used to tag packages that contain definitions of a certain pattern's UML-F pattern tags. In other words, *pattern packages* group all tags of a certain pattern.

In addition to the metamodel elements shown in figure 2.6 on the previous page, the *UML-F Foundation profile* defines a set of OCL constraints as shown in listing 2.1:

Listing 2.1: *UML-F Foundation profile* OCL constraints

```
1  -- Expansion strings have to be valid tag definitions
2  context TagDef inv:
3    self.expansion->forAll( e |
4        Profiles::Stereotype.allInstances->exists( s |
5          ( s.isStereotyped("TagDef") or
6              s.isStereotyped("PatternTagDef"))
7            and e = s.name ))
8
9  -- Pattern tags have to be defined in the namespace of a pattern
10 context Profiles::Stereotype inv:
11   self.isStereotyped("PatternTagDef") implies
12     self.allNamespaces()->select( ns |
13       ns.isStereotyped("Pattern"))->notEmpty()
14
15 -- PatternTags have to be stereotyped accordingly
16 context PatternTag inv:
17   self.isStereotyped("PatternTagDef")
18
```

```
19  -- PatternTagDefs have to use PatternDef as base class
20  context Profiles::Stereotype inv:
21    self.isStereotyped("PatternTagDef") implies
22      self.oclIsKindOf(PatternTag)
23
24  -- Auxiliary operation to determine stereotype extension
25  -- (taken from [Ziadi et al., 2003])
26  context ModelElement::isStereotyped(S : String) : Boolean
27  post : result =
28    self.stereotype->exists( s | s.name = S)
```

These constraints ensure the consistency of the metamodel defined by any profile that defines UML-F tags. The four invariants guarantee that:

1. For every expansion tagged value of a UML-F tag definition, there exists another UML-F tag definition named accordingly.

2. Every UML-F pattern tag is defined in the namespace of a pattern package, i.e. in a package stereotyped «*Pattern*».

3. Stereotypes derived from the PatternTag metaclass have to be stereotyped «*PatternTagDef*». In other words, every stereotype derived from PatternTag has to define a UML-F pattern tag.

4. Every definition of a UML-F pattern tag has to use PatternTag as base class.

The auxiliary operation isStereotyped provides a convenient way to find out if a model element has a certain stereotype. It is taken from Ziadi et al. [ZJF03, appendix A.1].

2.2.5   The UML-F Library Profile

Essential construction principles, design patterns, and domain specific patterns form a hierarchy of framework building blocks. The *UML-F Library profile* uses a layering approach to organize the tags into categories, as shown in figure 2.5 on page 40. Each tag layer serves a certain documentation purpose:

Basic modeling tag layer: Basic properties of model elements, such as adaptation flexibility and framework relevancy, are described with basic modeling tags. Since these tags are of a very mechanical nature they do not reveal information about the intentions of the framework's developers.

Essential construction principles layer: Tags residing in this layer are arranged in groups of related tags that are used to document a certain construction principle. They annotate the roles that classes, methods, and objects play in these fundamental framework building blocks. Essential construction principles tags usually rely on basic modeling tags.

Pattern layer: Based on the essential construction principles tags, the design pattern tags are defined. Design patterns are more specialized than construction principles and usually consist of more roles than their base construction principle. Thus, not all pattern tags expand to construction principles tags.

A Tabular Template For Defining UML-F Tags

The subsequent sections list the tags for each layer of figure 2.5 on page 40 and discuss further details. Tags are introduced in a tabular form using a template, which is an adapted form of the template used in the original UML-F profile [FPR01]. The meaning of the columns is defined as follows:

Tag name*: Defines a descriptive name for the tag. Tag aliases are specified in parentheses. In terms of the UML profile, the tag name is the name of the stereotype metaclass. The aliases are specified in the tagged value alias, as defined in figure 2.6 on page 41.

Applies to*: Lists the model element types the tag may be applied to. This specifies the metaclasses in the UML profile the stereotype is associated to by using the *extension* relationship.

Expansion: Lists the tags the newly introduced tag can be expanded to. In the UML profile, this property is specified in the tagged value expansion, as defined in figure 2.6 on page 41.

Pattern Tag: Specifies whether the tag is a pattern tag. In the UML profile, this property specifies if the tag is defined using the «*TagDef*» stereotype or the «*Pattern-TagDef*» stereotype. When it is clear from the context whether a tag is part of a pattern or not, this column might be omitted.

Description: Explains the meaning of the tag when attached to a model element.

Columns marked with an asterisk * are mandatory columns, whereas unmarked columns are optional and are not used in all tag definitions.

2.2.6   Basic Modeling Layer Tags

The main purpose of basic modeling layer tags is the documentation of basic framework concepts. They communicate the intended use of framework elements and thus provide a notation for the framework developer to give the framework user guidance for the adaptation process. Furthermore, they enhance the communication among framework developers as they document general design intentions. All basic modeling tags are defined using the «TagDef» stereotype.

Basic Template-Hook Tags

Template- and hook-methods and classes are the fundamental building blocks of adaptable object-oriented software. They are arranged in a certain way to attain a specific adaptability behavior. UML-F introduces the tags in table 2.1 for the explicit documentation of both roles.

Table 2.1: Basic Template-Hook tags

Tag name	Applies to	Description
«Template» («T»)	Class	The class contains a template method.
«template» («t»)	Operation	The operation is a template method and thus is responsible to call the corresponding hook method, according to a predefined protocol.
«Hook» («H»)	Class Interface	The model element contains a hook method.
«hook» («h»)	Operation	The operation is a hook method, called by the corresponding template method.

Figure 2.7 on the following page depicts how the tags presented in table 2.1 can be defined using the graphical UML 2.0 notation. In the remainder of this section, basic modeling layer tags are defined in the tabular notation only. The graphical notation can easily be derived in analogy to this example.

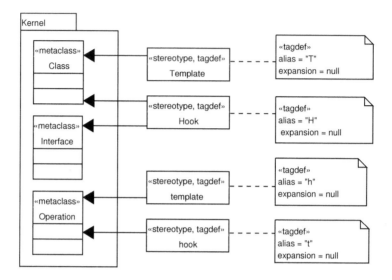

Figure 2.7: Basic Template-Hook tag definition

Relevancy Tags

Table 2.2 shows the relevancy tags, which are used to depict the relevancy of a model element to the framework, to an application build on top of the framework, to a utility library, or to the runtime system.

Table 2.2: Relevancy tags

Tag name	Applies to	Description
«application»	Class Package Interface	The model element is an application element. It does not belong to the framework.
«framework»	Class Package Interface	The model element is part of the framework.

Table 2.2: Relevancy tags (continued)

Tag name	Applies to	Description
«*utility*»	Class Package Interface	The model element is part of a utility library, or it is part of the runtime system.

Adaptation Tags

The so-called *adaptation tags* are shown in table 2.3. These tags express whether the model element can be adapted for the purpose of framework instantiation. If adaptation is possible, they further specify which level of freedom for the adaptation can be used: either static adaptation at design time, or dynamic adaptation at runtime.

Since most of the methods in a framework are not intended to be adapted, the «*fixed*» tag is defined as default tag. In addition, this convention introduces an additional level of security to the profile, since intended adaptability has to be enabled explicitly.

Table 2.3: Adaptation tags

Tag name	Applies to	Description
«*fixed*»	Class Operation	The model element is fixed; it may not be changed by subclassing. Methods may not be changed in subclasses and it is not allowed to add new subclasses to fixed generalizations.
«*adapt-static*»	Class Interface Operation	The model element can be adapted statically during design time by subclassing or interface realization. During runtime the model element is fixed.
«*adapt-dyn*»	Class Interface Operation	The model element can be adapted dynamically at runtime. Dynamic loading of new subclasses, for example, is allowed.

2.2.7   Essential Construction Principles Layer Tags

The tags residing in the essential construction principles layer are used to denote the application of essential construction principles, as described in section 1.1.1, in a particular framework part. Groups of tags are used in order to specify the roles that the model elements play in the corresponding essential construction principle. Figure 2.8 shows the package structure. Each construction principle is defined as a separate *pattern package* containing the corresponding tag definitions.

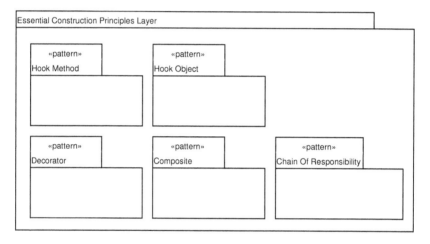

Figure 2.8: Essential construction principles layer structure

Since in a framework many instances of a construction principle may be used, it is important to be able to quickly identify the group an essential construction principle tag belongs to. For that purpose, the tags in this layer are all defined as «*PatternTagDef*». This implies that the stereotype metaclasses are subclasses of PatternTag (cf. section 2.2.4), and thus have the tagged value instance defined. The value assigned to instance specifies the name of the construction principle's instance.

Hook-Method Tags

Table 2.4 on the next page defines the tags used for denoting an instance of the Hook-Method construction principle. All three tags residing in the Hook-Method pattern package have to be used together to validly represent a Hook-Method instance.

Table 2.4: Hook-Method tags

Tag name	Applies to	Expansion	Description
«HookM-TH» («HM-TH», «TH»)	Class	«Template», «Hook»	The class represents an instance of the Hook-Method construction principle.
«HookM-t» («HM-t»)	Operation	«template»	The method plays the template role in the instance of the Hook-Method construction principle.
«HookM-h» («HM-h»)	Operation	«hook»	The method plays the hook role in the instance of Hook-Method construction principle.

Figure 2.9 on the following page shows the graphical UML 2.0 notation that is equivalent to the tag definition given in table 2.4. Note that the inheritance relation to PatternTag is necessary since the tags are defined using «PatternTagDef».

The application of the Hook-Method UML-F tags is best illustrated by using the principle's structure itself. Figure 2.10 on the following page depicts how the tags are used.

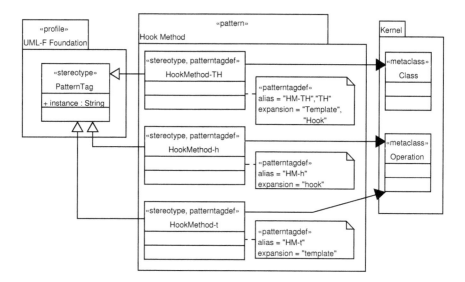

Figure 2.9: Hook Method tag definition

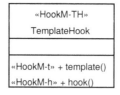

Figure 2.10: Hook Method structure and UML-F tags

Hook-Object Tags

The tags used to denote an instance of the Hook-Object construction principle are defined in table 2.5. The four tags have to be used together to validly represent a Hook-Object instance. They reside in the Hook-Object package.

Table 2.5: Hook-Object tags

Tag name	Applies to	Expansion	Description
«HookObj-T» («HO-T»)	Class	«Template»	The class contains the template method.
«HookObj-H» («HO-H»)	Class Interface	«Hook»	The model element plays the role of the hook object. It contains the definition of the hook method, which is called by the template method.
«HookObj-t» («HO-t»)	Operation	«template»	The method plays the template role.
«HookObj-h» («HO-h»)	Operation	«hook»	The method plays the hook role.
«HookObj-Ref» («HO-Ref»)	Association	—	The association models the reference to the hook object.

Figure 2.11 on the following page shows the equivalent graphical notation. Note that the inheritance relations to PatternTag are not shown for the purpose of clearness.

The application of the Hook Object UML-F tags is best shown by using the principle's structure itself. Figure 2.12 on the next page depicts how the tags are used.

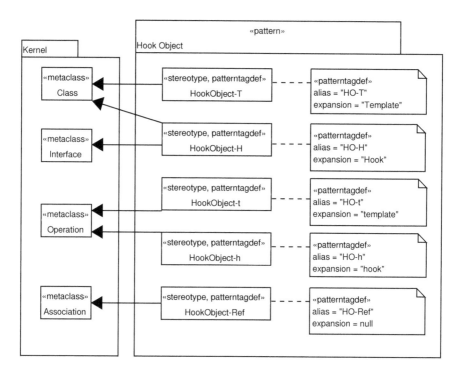

Figure 2.11: Hook Object tag definition

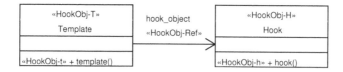

Figure 2.12: Hook Object structure and UML-F tags

Chain-Of-Responsibility Tags

Table 2.6 defines the tags used for denoting an instance of the Chain-Of-Responsibility construction principle. The three tags have to be used together to validly represent a Chain-Of-Responsibility instance.

Table 2.6: Chain-Of-Responsibility tags

Tag name	Applies to	Expansion	Description
«COR-TH»	Class	«Template», «Hook»	The class contains the template-hook method.
«COR-th»	Operation	«template», «hook»	The method is the template-hook method. It is responsible for recursively iterating through the chain.
«COR-successor»	Association	—	The association models the reference to the next chain element.

The equivalent graphical notation to table 2.6 is shown in figure 2.13 on the following page. For the purpose of brevity, the inheritance relations to PatternTag are not shown in the diagram.

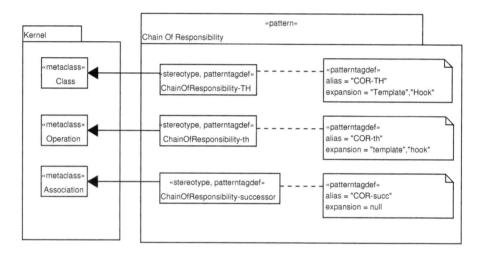

Figure 2.13: Chain Of Responsibility tag definition

Composite Tags

The tags used to denote an instance of the Composite construction principle are defined in table 2.7. The six tags have to be used together to validly represent a Composite instance.

Table 2.7: Composite tags

Tag name	Applies to	Expansion	Description
«Composite-T» (*«Comp-T»*)	Class Interface	«Template»	Denotes the template class containing the template method. The template class plays the *Composite* role. Composites have children and are responsible for traversing the tree structure in a recursive manner.
«Composite-H» (*«Comp-H»*)	Class	«Hook»	The class contains the hook method and plays the *Component* role. The component declares the common interface for all objects in the composition.
«Composite-Leaf» (*«Comp-Leaf»*)	Class	«Hook»	Denotes a *Leaf* class. Leaf classes contain hook methods.
«Composite-t» (*«Comp-t»*)	Operation	«template»	The method plays the template role and traverses the tree structure.
«Composite-h» (*«Comp-h»*)	Operation	«hook»	The method plays the hook role.
«Composite-children» (*«Comp-children»*)	Association	—	The association models the reference to the children of a composite node in the tree structure.

Decorator Tags

Table 2.8 defines the tags used for denoting an instance of the Decorator construction principle.
The five tags have to be used together to validly represent a Decorator instance.

Table 2.8: Decorator tags

Tag name	Applies to	Expansion	Description
«Decorator-T» (« Dec-T»)	Class	«Template»	The class is the template class playing the *Decorator* role and containing the template method.
«Decorator-H» (« Dec-H»)	Class Interface	«Hook»	Denotes the hook class that plays the *Component* role. This class contains the hook method.
«Decorator-t» (« Dec-t»)	Operation	«template»	The method is the template method responsible to call the hook method.
«Decorator-h» (« Dec-t»)	Operation	«hook»	The method plays the hook role.
«Decorator-comp» (« Dec-comp»)	Association	—	The association models the reference to the hook class (*component*).

2.2.8   Patterns Layer Tags

The UML-F Library profile's uppermost layer consists of tags for the denotation of design
patterns and domain specific patterns.

Design patterns as well as domain specific patterns may be dependent upon essential construction principles or other patterns. Consequently, design pattern tags and domain specific pattern
tags may be extended to the corresponding essential construction principles tags and design
pattern tags.

In the Pattern Layer package, every pattern is grouped in a separate *pattern package*. In accor-
dance with section 1.1.2, all design patterns relevant for framework construction are supported:

- Abstract Factory

- Bridge

- Builder

- Chain of Responsibility

- Command

- Composite

- Decorator

- Factory Method

- Interpreter

- Observer

- Prototype

- State

- Strategy

- Template Method

The Observer pattern is used to illustrate the definition of UML-F pattern for a design pattern. Tags for the other design patterns are defined analogously. Table 2.9 shows the Observer pattern's tag definition.

Since the Observer pattern is based on the Hook-Object construction principle, as discussed in sections 1.1.1 and 1.1.2, the Observer tags expand to the corresponding Hook-Object tags.

Table 2.9: Observer tags

Tag name	Applies to	Expansion	Description
«Observer-Subject» (≪Obs-Subj≫)	Class Interface	≪HookObj-T≫	The model element plays the *Subject* role in the pattern instance.

Table 2.9: Observer tags (continued)

Tag name	Applies to	Expansion	Description
«Observer-Observer» («Obs-Obs»)	Class Interface	«HookObj-H»	The model element plays the *Observer* role in the pattern instance.
«Observer-ConcrObserver» («Obs-CObs»)	Class	—	The class is a *Concrete observer*.
«Observer-notify» («Obs-ntfy»)	Operation	«HookObj-t»	The method plays the role of the *notification* method in the pattern instance.
«Observer-update» («Obs-upd»)	Operation	«HookObj-h»	The method defines the *update* method.
«Observer-concreteupdate» («Obs-cupd»)	Operation	—	This is the concrete implementation of the *update* method.
«Observer-observers» («Obs-obsvs»)	Association	«HookObj-Ref»	The association models the reference to the observers attached to the subject.

Figure 2.14 on the facing page shows how the tags defined tabular form can be defined using the graphical notation. For the purpose of brevity, the inheritance relations to PatternTag are not shown in the diagram.

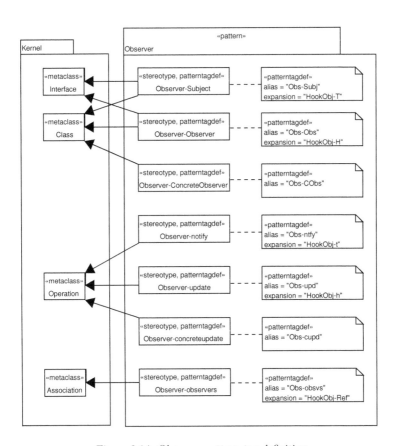

Figure 2.14: Observer pattern tag definition

An example of how to apply the UML-F tags is shown in figure 2.15.

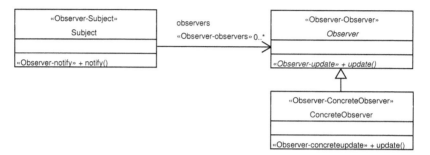

Figure 2.15: Observer structure and UML-F tags

UML-F tags for the remaining design patterns are defined similarly to the tags for the Observer pattern. The complete list of UML-F tags is given in appendix A on page 171.

2.2.9   An Exemplary UML-F Profile Application

The purpose of this section is to illustrate the application of UML-F tags. As an example the Observer pattern, whose UML-F tags were introduced in the previous section 2.2.8, is used.

A simple queue in a simulation environment (SimulationQueue) acts as Subject in the example. Whenever the state of the queue changes, all registered queueObservers are notified. The Observers have to be subclasses of the abstract class *SimulationQueueObserver*, which plays the pattern's *Observer* role. Two ConcreteObservers, namely GUIObserver responsible for visualizing the queue's content and QueueStatisticsObserver that calculates statistics of the queue, are part of the example model as well. Figure 2.16 on the next page shows the example model, already annotated with the Observer UML-F tags.

Figure 2.17 on the facing page shows the same class model, annotated with the Observer pattern's essential construction principles layer expansion. See table 2.9 on page 57 or figure 2.14 on the preceding page for details of the expansion relation.

2.2.10   UML-F Profile Notes

The UML-F profile proposes the usage of a subset of the Unified Modeling Language, which has proven its usefulness in framework development projects. Namely, class and object diagrams are used for describing the framework's static structure. Sequence diagrams and collaboration

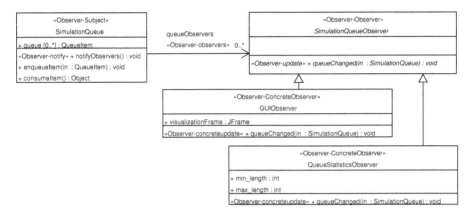

Figure 2.16: Observer example for UML-F tags – Pattern layer

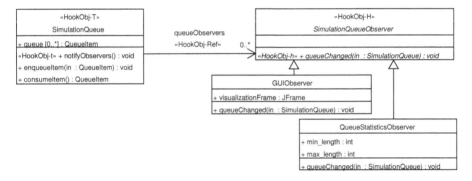

Figure 2.17: Observer example for UML-F tags – Construction Principles layer

diagrams describe behavioral aspects. As a matter of fact, any other diagram that is part of the language standard may be used, too. The proposed partition is a suggestion stemming from practical framework project experiences. UML-F does not focus on requirements engineering or on distribution; some of the skipped UML diagrams mostly deal with these issues.

Standard UML concepts are defined to be more specific when used with the profile. First, all classes are considered to be implementation classes. Second, the primary form of object interaction is the method call. Third, object compositions are based on associations, where an additional dependency on the lifetimes of the associated objects comes into consideration.

The *principle of underspecification* is applied consistently when working with models that use the UML-F profile. This principle states that one can not draw any conclusions about the implementation from information not included in the model. If a model is complete it has to be marked appropriately.

CHAPTER 3

UML-F Tool Vision: The *PANEX* Project

Framework development and framework adaption are complex and demanding tasks. Comprehensive domain knowledge and the ability to abstract from unnecessary details, without leaving out essential aspects, is indispensable for the framework developer to be able to define appropriate abstractions. These abstractions manifest in architectural design decisions. Efficient communication is needed to share knowledge about these concepts among development peers, and for this purpose framework documentation plays an important role.

Application developers utilizing frameworks need to learn the framework abstractions and component interaction patterns. The framework documentation should communicate these concepts effectively. The success of the adaptation to a great part relies on the developer's ability to identify suitable framework hot spots.

Developers dealing with frameworks, whether building or using them, need adequate tools at hand that support them for their specific tasks. UML-F is an approach to improve the expressivity of UML diagrams, in order to provide a compact representation of design intentions. Explicitly marking the usages of essential framework construction principles and design patterns highlights the framework's hot spots.

The *Pattern Annotation Extension (PANEX)* project, which is a major topic of this book, aims at providing tool support for UML-F. PANEX, however, not only implements the UML-F profile, it also provides alternative visualizations and design tools. Although not strictly conform to the UML standard, these extension provide an extra added value for users in the framework domain.

This chapter explains the tool vision which served as the statement of user needs for the PANEX project. First, general requirements for a tool that supports framework development are described, and the problem areas in that domain are identified. Second, possible user roles are identified. Finally, a list of must-have features is presented, which depicts the main concerns the tool has to deal with. For each feature, solution alternatives are discussed from the tool user's point of view.

3.1 Requirements for Adequate Tool Support

For the success of a software development tool it is essential to consider the application domain's peculiarities, and to pinpoint the specific aspects the tool is aimed at. This section presents a model of potential problem areas in the framework domain. Based on that model, the tool's primary responsibilities are defined.

3.1.1 Framework Related Problem Areas

Traditional object-oriented design languages do not provide constructs for representing flexibility and variability requirements [FPR00]. UML-F addresses these problems by handling variation points as first-class citizens, which makes the intention behind a certain design decision explicit. Thus, a UML-F based tool could help to document framework design decisions.

In his thesis, Viljamaa presents a model of the main problems in software development related to frameworks [Vil01, p. 39 ff]. Table 3.1 on the next page arranges these problem areas according to the different phases of framework development and application development.

A tool based on UML-F can not address all these problem areas. The following paragraphs describe in which of these areas the PANEX tool can provide help:

- By its very nature, the Unified Modeling Language is tied to describing software designs. For that reason, also the UML-F approach is best suited for describing the framework design. Thus, problem *(3)* is a potential candidate to be supported by PANEX.

- UML-F descriptions emphasize the hot spots of the framework design. The essence of framework documentation is the description of these variation points and their adaption. Therefore PANEX can aid developers to deal with problems *(5)* and *(8)*.

- Evaluation of potential framework candidates for a particular software project partly relies on the availability of the provided variation points. Hence, the usage of UML-F in

Table 3.1: Main problems areas of software development with frameworks

	Domain Analysis	**Design**	**Implementation**	**Maintenance**
FW Development	*(1)* How to determine hot spots?	*(2)* How to design hot spots? *(3)* How to describe the design?	*(4)* How to implement hot spots? *(5)* How to document the framework?	*(6)* How to manage changes in domain and hot spot requirements?
Appl. Development		*(7)* How to choose an appropriate framework?	*(8)* How to specialize the framework?	*(9)* How to manage changes in application domain requirements?

high level design diagrams can aid in the decision process, i.e. with problem *(7)*. This problem, however, is not a major concern of PANEX.

3.1.2   PANEX User Roles

Software development with frameworks involves different user roles. This section identifies the roles important for the PANEX project. On top of these roles, possible stakeholders of the PANEX tool are determined.

Section 1.2.2 describes the roles involved in the framework development and evolution process: *framework developer, component developer, application developer,* and *end user.* The tool does not just support framework development, but also framework documentation. Thus, possible audience roles for the documentation as described in section 1.2.3 also are important for the tool: *decision maker, framework user,* and *framework expert.*

Some of these roles resemble other roles or parts of them. For that reason, new roles based on the ones listed above are described:

Application Developer: An application developer uses the framework and the components based on the framework to build application programs. The *PANEX application developer* role thus corresponds to the *application developer* (development) and the *framework user* (documentation) roles.

Framework Developer: A framework developer designs, implements, or changes the framework. In addition, the framework developer develops components based on the framework that can easily be used for application development. The *PANEX framework developer* role thus includes the development roles *framework developer* and *component developer*.

In order to be able to accomplish this task, an in-depth understanding of the framework internals, design knowledge, and domain knowledge has to be acquired. Since this role may change the framework implementation, it is also responsible for keeping the design documents up to date. Thus, the *PANEX framework developer* role matches with the *framework expert* documentation role.

Pattern Developer: The pattern developer's main responsibility is to develop and refine domain specific patterns. It is a *framework developer* with advanced knowledge of design patterns and extensible software architectures, and has experience in the problem domain. A developer capable of creating domain specific patterns usually has been part of several framework projects in the problem domain.

The PANEX project does not take the *end user* development role into consideration, because an end user usually is not concerned with the internals of the application program.

The documentation role *decision maker* also is not explicitly taken into account. For the technical part of a framework decision, the decision maker can impersonate the role of a *high level application developer* evaluating the framework's technical feasibility. The provision of documentation at such a level of abstraction is not a primary concern for the PANEX tool.

The *pattern developer* role is newly introduced since one of the main building blocks of the PANEX project is the support of domain specific patterns.

3.2   Tool Features

All features described in this section are must-have features. In other words, the PANEX tool has to provide support for all features discussed here. Every must-have feature is documented by a subsection describing the problem situation and a second subsection proposing possible solutions.

3.2.1   Visualization of UML-F Tags

Problem Description

For a tool that employs the UML-F profile, the most essential feature is the visualization of UML-F tags. UML-F tags can be visualized in various ways. One critical aspect here is to prevent *overloading* of the diagrams with unnecessary details. On the other hand, all necessary details have to be part of the visualization, such that the connections between the framework classes and the underlying patterns and construction principles are highlighted.

Solution Proposals

Three different solution proposals have been identified:

1. *UML-F stereotype notation:*

   The first solution proposal is to use the stereotype notation as defined in the UML-F specification. Figure 3.1 shows an example.

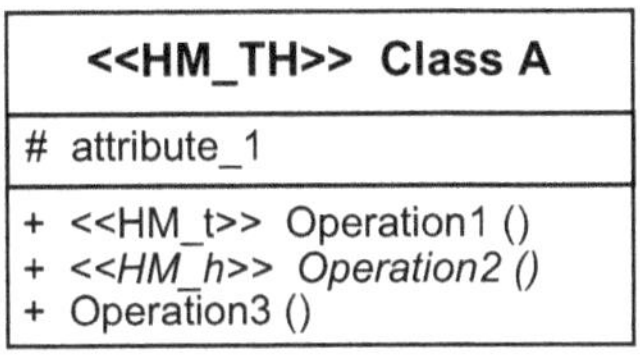

<<HM_TH>> Class A
attribute_1
+ <<HM_t>> Operation1 () + *<<HM_h>> Operation2 ()* + Operation3 ()

   Figure 3.1: UML-F stereotype notation

   This is a straightforward way of visualizing tags since it is completely UML compliant. Nevertheless, it has some shortcomings. The intermixing of standard UML model elements and UML-F tag stereotypes soon becomes very complex and makes large diagrams hard to understand. Although the two class diagrams in figure 2.16 on page 61 and figure 2.17 on page 61 are not very complex, it is easy to see that the UML-F tags introduce a complexity of their own. Moreover, when two or more pattern instances are shown in a single diagram, the diagram becomes more complicated.

2. *Pattern mapping notation:*

   Another solution proposal is based on the emphasis of how model elements map to the corresponding pattern elements. The basic idea is to show the pattern's structure in the same diagram as the framework classes based on the pattern. Arrows are used to depict the relations between framework model elements and pattern model elements. Figure 3.2 on the next page shows the mapping notation.

   The pattern mapping notation is based on the notation used in the original UML-F profile to depict the mapping between construction principles and framework classes [FPR01, chapter 4].

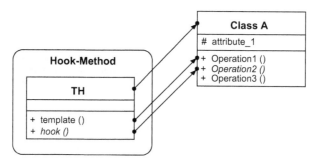

Figure 3.2: Pattern mapping notation

3. *Pattern marker notation:*

The introduction of markers solves the intermixing problem discovered in the first solution. A marker consists of the UML-F tag name, and is located next to the corresponding model element outside the class boundary. Thus, markers are clearly separated from standard UML model elements in the diagram. Figure 3.3 shows a sketch of how a visualization can look like.

TH

Class A

attribute_1

t + Operation1 ()
h + *Operation2 ()*
      + Operation3 ()

Figure 3.3: Pattern marker notation

This notation is well suited for highlighting the pattern roles of methods and classes. In particular, the marking of template and hook roles can be done in a very clear and intuitive way.

A drawback of this solution is that it is not intended to show more than one pattern for a certain class or to mark associations. For that reason, this solution is complementary to the other solution proposals.

The pattern marker notation is based on the notation used by Pree to highlight template and hook roles in class diagrams [PP04, chapter 5].

3.2.2   Support of Tag-Groups

Problem Description

Frameworks usually are built using several instances of patterns and essential construction principles. Since one pattern usually is represented by several UML-F tags, the tags part of a certain pattern instance form a *tag group*, as defined in section 2.2.7.

The tool has to support UML-F tag groups considering the following aspects:

- *Management:* Tags groups can be created, renamed, deleted.

- *Visualization:* All tags of a group can be visualized, which has already been discussed in the previous section 3.2.1.

- *Selective marking:* Tag groups in diagrams can be shown or hidden selectively.

Solution Proposal

The management and mark functionalities can be realized by an integrated management tool. The tool should seamlessly integrate in the modeling environment and enable the user to manage tag groups. In addition, tag groups of an active diagram can be marked or unmarked. A possible implementation might arrange the tag groups in a tree-like manner corresponding to the UML-F tag layers.

3.2.3   Moving Between Layers

Problem Description

A similar problem to the tag group issue described in the previous section 3.2.2 is the support for tag layering. As described in section 2.5 on page 40, the UML-F profile is arranged in layers. For a better understanding and overview it is useful to visualize only a certain UML-F layer in a diagram. For instance, one user might want to see just the template-hook roles for a complex domain specific pattern, while another user might be interested in the detailed pattern roles. The PANEX tool should allow for such a selective and layer dependent representation of tag groups.

The Observer example in section 2.2.9 already provides an example for this feature: Figure 2.16 on page 61 shows the UML-F tags for the Observer pattern. The corresponding UML-F tags at the essential construction principles layer are show in figure 2.17 on page 61.

Solution Proposal

The integrated tool could be used to allow the user to perform the selection of a certain UML-F layer, which then manifests in a changed diagram view of the corresponding model elements.

3.2.4   Pattern Annotation Procedure

Problem Description

A critical aspect for the success of the UML-F tool is the usability of the pattern annotation procedure. An awkward and troublesome user interface discourages developers to use the tool, and it results in a high learning curve.

Solution Proposal

A possible solution to this problem is to provide a wizard for the annotation. The wizard might be organized such that the parameters needed to perform the pattern instantiation are collected from the user in a systematic way. The choices to be made by the user should be represented in a clear and simple way.

3.2.5   Support of Domain Specific Patterns

Problem Description

UML-F allows the definition of new patterns specific to the framework's problem domain. The tool should enable domain experts to manage domain specific patterns, which includes the following tasks:

- *Management:* Domain specific patterns can be created, modified and deleted.

- *Documentation:* Documentation possibilities are available to enrich the plain pattern definitions.

- *Annotation:* The new patterns can be integrated easily in the annotation procedure.

- *Visualization:* It is possible to visualize domains specific patterns in the same way as for other design patterns.

Solution Proposal

A straightforward solution approach is to use the mechanisms of the underlying CASE tool to define the whole UML-F pattern set. This, for instance, can be achieved by using class diagrams to represent the pattern's static structure. Behavioral diagrams can document the interactions between pattern participants. The pattern annotation wizard can dynamically collect the required instantiation parameters and perform the annotation.

For that solution to be applicable, it might be necessary to introduce certain restrictions or extensions to the diagram notation for pattern definitions.

Part II

ArgoUML Featuring PANEX

Development of an UML-F Extension to ArgoUML

CHAPTER 4

PANEX Software Requirements

In the previous chapter 3, the user needs for a UML-F based tool are stated. Based on them, essential software requirements for the tool can be identified.

This chapter uses *Use Cases (UC)* to capture functional requirements. In several software processes, use cases established as the main method for requirements engineering. The *Rational Unified Process (RUP)*, for example, uses a process model that is use case centric, and also architecture centric [Kru00, Lar01]. In RUP, the development process primarily is driven by use cases, which are used to describe all system requirements. In every process step, such as architecture design, implementation, or testing, the focus is on the correct fulfillment of the requirements stated in form of use cases. Also in the *Object Engineering Process (OEP)* a use case based approach for capturing functional requirements is employed [Oes01].

Informally, use cases are *"stories of using a system"* [Lar01]. A use case is defined as set of actions that, when executed following one after another in sequence, form a certain behavior of the system to be modeled [JRH+03]. A use case is triggered, i.e. it is instantiated, by an actor, and results in a certain result of functional value.

The use-case model, which is the set of all use cases of a system and their relations, models the system's environment and functionality. In other words, the collection of use cases can be seen as the specification of the system's behavior that captures *all and only* the behaviors related to satisfying the system stakeholders' interests [Lar01].

This chapter describes the requirements for the PANEX tool. First, functional requirements are described by developing the use-case model. The use cases for every stakeholder are shown in separate use case diagrams. Based on these diagrams, every use case is described in detail. Second, nonfunctional requirements are identified and described.

4.1 Functional Requirements

According to the IEEE Guide to the Software Engineering Body of Knowledge, *"Functional requirements describe the functions that the software is to execute; for example, formatting some text or modulating a signal. They are sometimes known as capabilities"* [SWE04, chapter 2.1.3].

This section describes the functional requirements for the PANEX tool. For this purpose use cases are used, which are presented in separate use case diagrams for each actor. Some actors are be associated to the same use cases, so all use case diagrams are presented before each use case is described in detail. Use cases are described in a tabular form, which is based on the tables proposed by Wirfs-Brock and McKean [WBM02] and by Oesterreich [Oes01].

4.1.1 PANEX Actors

The basis for any use case model is to identify the system's actors. The results of the PANEX user needs analysis described in section 3.1.2 can be reused for this purpose. The three stakeholders identified there can be seen in figure 4.1: *Application Developer*, *Framework Developer*, and *Pattern Developer*.

Figure 4.1: PANEX Actors

4.1.2 Application Developer Use Cases

The application developer is the framework's user, building applications based on the framework to be documented using the PANEX tool. Figure 4.2 on the next page shows the use case diagram depicting the use cases this actor is associated to.

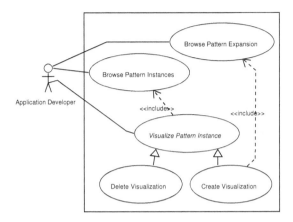

Figure 4.2: Application developer use cases

4.1.3 Framework Developer Use Cases

The framework developer, as described in section 3.1.2 on page 65, is the framework's main architect and developer. As can be seen in figure 4.3 on the next page, the use cases associated to the framework developer for the most part are related to the documentation of the design decisions that drive the framework development.

4.1.4 Pattern Developer Use Cases

A pattern developer in the first place is responsible for the creation and improvement of domain specific design patterns. Figure 4.4 on page 79 shows the corresponding use case diagram.

4.1.5 Use Case Descriptions

This section provides detailed descriptions of the use cases presented in figures 4.2 to 4.4 on pages 77–79. They are described using a tabular form, which is based on the tables proposed by Wirfs-Brock and McKean [WBM02] and by Oesterreich [Oes01]. The meaning of the table rows is described as follows:

Use Case: The use case's unique name and number.

Actors: This is the list of stakeholders, i.e. the list of all actors associated to the use case. It is important to specify all stakeholders of a use case

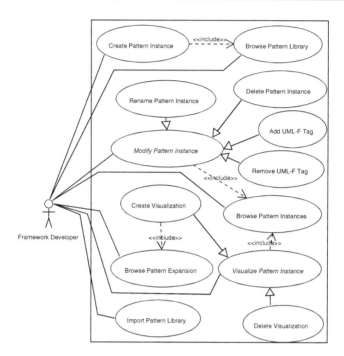

Figure 4.3: Framework developer use cases

explicitly, since the use case implementation should satisfy the interests of all stakeholders.

Description: This brief description is the use case's tag line. It explains the use case's purpose in one sentence.

Preconditions: Preconditions state what *must always* be true before a use case scenario can begin.

Success Guarantee: Success guarantees, or *postconditions*, describe what must be true after successful completion of a use case scenario. It does not matter whether the basic path or one of the alternative paths has been taken.

Basic Flow: This scenario, also called the *main success scenario* or *happy path scenario*, describes the typical success scenario, and has to meet the needs of all stakeholders.

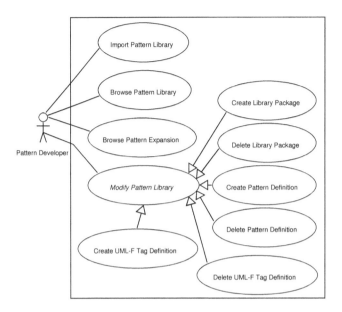

Figure 4.4: Pattern developer use cases

Alternative Flows: Alternative flows describe all other scenarios that are not included in the main success scenario, both success and failure. Alternative flows are branches from the basic flow.

Design Notes: This section contains hints for the use case implementation as well as notes on decisions made when designing the use case model.

The following tables 4.1 to 4.20 on pages 79–90 describe the use cases identified in the previous sections.

Table 4.1: Description of UC1 – Browse pattern instances

Use Case	UC1 – Browse pattern instances
Actors	Application Developer, Framework Developer
Description	Provide a user interface for browsing all pattern instances.
Preconditions	At least one pattern instance exists.
Success Guarantee	—

Table 4.1: Descr. of UC1 – Browse pattern instances
(cont.)

Basic Flow	1. The user interface shows all pattern instances.
	2. When the user selects a certain pattern instance, detailed information about the corresponding model elements and their UML-F tags are shown.
Alternative Flows	3. When the user interface is used to select a certain pattern instance, i.e. when this use case is used in the context of *UC3* or *UC8*, a pattern instance has to be selected to finish the scenario wit success.
Design Notes	This UC is included in use cases *UC3* and *UC8* for the purpose of selecting a certain pattern instance. In this situation, the pattern instance selected by the user has to be stored for later use.

Table 4.2: Description of UC2 – Browse pattern expansion

Use Case	UC2 – Browse pattern expansion
Actors	Application Developer, Framework Developer, Pattern Developer
Description	Provide a user interface for browsing the expansion relations of the UML-F tags that belong to a certain pattern.
Preconditions	The model contains at least one UML-F tag.
Success Guarantee	—
Basic Flow	1. The user interface shows all patterns and UML-F tags defined in the model.
	2. When the user selects a certain pattern or UML-F tag, the patterns / UML-F tags it expands to are shown.
	3. This can be repeated until the model contains no further expansion relation for the selected UML-F element.
Alternative Flows	1a. When this UC is included in use case *UC4* for the purpose of selecting the expansion layer for a given pattern, only the this pattern is shown as root for the expansion tree.

Table 4.2: Descr. of UC2 – Browse pattern expansion
(cont.)

Design Notes	This UC is included in use case *UC4* for the purpose of selecting a certain expansion layer for a given pattern. In this situation, the expansion layer selected by the user has to be stored for later use. A tree-like user interface seems most appropriate for browsing the expansion tree.

Table 4.3: Description of UC3 – Visualize pattern instance

Use Case	UC3 – Visualize pattern instance
Actors	Application Developer, Framework Developer
Description	Abstract use case for the modification of a certain pattern instance's visualization.
Preconditions	The model contains at least one pattern instance.
Success Guarantee	—
Basic Flow	1. Select a pattern instance (includes *UC1*). 2. Modify the visualization (abstract step). 3. Update the user interface.
Alternative Flows	—
Design Notes	Includes use case *UC1*.

Table 4.4: Description of UC4 – Create visualization

Use Case	UC4 – Create visualization
Actors	Application Developer, Framework Developer
Description	Create a new visualization for a certain pattern instance and add it to the active diagram.
Preconditions	The model contains at least one pattern instance. A pattern instance has been selected (see base use case *UC3*). At least one model element that is tagged as instance of the selected pattern is shown in the active diagram.
Success Guarantee	A new visualization for the pattern instance has been created.

Table 4.4: Descr. of UC4 – Create visualization (cont.)

Basic Flow	(Implements step 2 of the super use case *UC3*)
	2a. Select the expansion layer for the selected pattern instance (includes *UC2*).
	2b. Select the visualization notation, e.g. the pattern mapping notation or the pattern marker notation.
	2c. Select the details to visualize, e.g. class roles, operation roles, or association roles.
	2d. Add the visualization to the active diagram.
Alternative Flows	2d$_1$. In case the pattern mapping notation is used, the user selects the diagram location where the pattern structure will be placed.
Design Notes	Includes use case *UC2*.

Table 4.5: Description of UC5 – Delete visualization

Use Case	UC5 – Delete visualization
Actors	Application Developer, Framework Developer
Description	Remove the visualization of a certain pattern instance from the active diagram.
Preconditions	The model contains at least one pattern instance.
	A pattern instance has been selected (see base use case *UC3*).
	The active diagram contains a visualization of the selected pattern instance.
Success Guarantee	The selected visualization has been removed.
Basic Flow	(Implements step 2 of the super use case *UC3*)
	2. Remove the visualization from the active diagram.
Alternative Flows	—
Design Notes	—

Table 4.6: Description of UC6 – Browse pattern library

Use Case	**UC6 – Browse pattern library**
Actors	Framework Developer, Pattern Developer
Description	Provide a user interface for browsing the complete UML-F library.
Preconditions	At least one library package is defined in the model.
Success Guarantee	—
Basic Flow	1. The user interface shows all UML-F library elements.
	2. When the user selects a certain pattern or tag, detailed information on that element is shown.
Alternative Flows	3. When the user interface is used to select a certain pattern, i.e. this use case is used in the context of *UC7*, a pattern has to be selected in order to be able to leave the user interface successfully.
Design Notes	This UC is included in use case *UC7* for the purpose of selecting a certain pattern. In this situation, the pattern selected by the user has to be stored for later use.
	A tree-like user interface seems most appropriate for browsing the UML-F library tree.

Table 4.7: Description of UC7 – Create pattern instance

Use Case	**UC7 – Create pattern instance**
Actor	Framework Developer
Description	Create an instance of a certain pattern.
Preconditions	A pattern with tags must be defined in the UML-F library.
Success Guarantee	The model elements that are part of the pattern instance have been tagged accordingly.
	New model elements have been created if necessary.

Table 4.7: Descr. of UC7 – Create pattern instance (cont.)

Basic Flow	1. The user selects a pattern (includes *UC6*).
	2. The user enters an instance name.
	3. Model elements are chosen that are part of the pattern instance, which can either be existing or new model elements.
	4. The new model elements are created.
	5. The model elements are tagged with the corresponding UML-F tags.
	6. Generalizations, realizations and dependencies that are not part of the model but that are specified in the UML-F pattern specification are generated.
Alternative Flows	—
Design Notes	Includes use case *UC6*.

Table 4.8: Description of UC8 – Modify pattern instance

Use Case	**UC8 – Modify pattern instance**
Actor	Framework Developer
Description	Abstract use case for the modification of a certain pattern instance.
Preconditions	At least one pattern instance exists.
Success Guarantee	—
Basic Flow	1. The user selects a pattern instance (includes UC1).
	2. The user selects the modification details (abstract step).
	3. The modification is performed.
Alternative Flows	—
Design Notes	Includes use case *UC1*.

Table 4.9: Description of UC9 – Rename pattern instance

Use Case	UC9 – Rename pattern instance
Actor	Framework Developer
Description	Change the name of a pattern instance.
Preconditions	At least one pattern instance exists.
	A pattern instance is selected (see super use case *UC8*).
Success Guarantee	The new name has been updated in all model elements that are part
	of the pattern instance.
Basic Flow	(Implements step 2 of the abstract use case *UC8*)
	2a. User enters the new instance name.
Alternative Flows	—
Design Notes	—

Table 4.10: Description of UC10 – Delete pattern instance

Use Case	UC10 – Delete pattern instance
Actor	Framework Developer
Description	Remove the selected pattern instance from the model.
Preconditions	At least one pattern instance exists.
	A pattern instance is selected (see super use case *UC8*).
Success Guarantee	The tags corresponding to the pattern instance have been removed
	from all model elements that are part of the pattern instance.
Basic Flow	(Implements step 2 of the abstract use case *UC8*)
	2a. The user has to re-confirm the deletion.
Alternative Flows	—
Design Notes	—

Table 4.11: Description of UC11 – Add UML-F tag

Use Case	UC11 – Add UML-F tag
Actor	Framework Developer
Description	Tag a model element with a UML-F tag as new part of a certain pattern instance.
Preconditions	At least one pattern instance exists.
	A pattern instance is selected (see super use case *UC8*).
Success Guarantee	The model element has been tagged as part of the pattern instance.
	If specified by the user, a new model element has been created.
Basic Flow	(Implements step 2 and overwrites step 3 of the abstract use case *UC8*)
	2a. The UML-F tag part of the pattern is chosen by the user.
	2b. The model element to be tagged is chosen by the user, which can either be an existing or a new model element.
	3a. Create the new model element if chosen by the user.
	3b. The model element is tagged with the chosen UML-F tag.
	3c. Generalizations, realizations and dependencies that are not part of the model but that are specified in the UML-F pattern specification are generated.
Alternative Flows	—
Design Notes	—

Table 4.12: Description of UC12 – Remove UML-F tag

Use Case	UC12 – Remove UML-F tag
Actor	Framework Developer
Description	Remove a UML-F tag from the model element that is part of a pattern instance and thus remove it from the pattern instance.
Preconditions	At least one pattern instance exists.
	A pattern instance is selected (see super use case *UC8*).
Success Guarantee	The UML-F tag has been removed from the selected model element.
Basic Flow	(Implements step 2 of the abstract use case *UC8*)
	2a. The model element and the corresponding UML-F tag are chosen.
Alternative Flows	—

Table 4.12: Descr. of UC12 – Remove UML-F tag (cont.)

Design Notes	—

Table 4.13: Description of UC13 – Import pattern library

Use Case	UC13 – Import pattern library
Actors	Framework Developer, Pattern Developer
Description	Import a pattern library to the current model.
Preconditions	—
Success Guarantee	The UML-F elements defined in the pattern library can be used in the model.
Basic Flow	1. The user selects a pattern library.
	2. The UML-F elements in the selected library are imported to the current model.
Alternative Flows	—
Design Notes	—

Table 4.14: Description of UC14 – Modify pattern library

Use Case	UC14 – Modify pattern library
Actor	Pattern Developer
Description	Abstract use case for the modification of the pattern library.
Preconditions	—
Success Guarantee	—
Basic Flow	1. Perform the modification (abstract step).
	2. Check the UML-F metamodel consistency.
	3. The library changes are immediately propagated to the PANEX user interface.
Alternative Flows	—
Design Notes	—

Table 4.15: Description of UC15 – Create library package

Use Case	UC15 – Create library package
Actor	Pattern Developer
Description	Create a new UML-F library package.
Preconditions	There is no package with an identical name in the same namespace.
Success Guarantee	A new package with the given name in the selected namespace has been created.
Basic Flow	(Implements step 1 of the abstract use case *UC14*)
	1a. The user selects the namespace, i.e. the model's root namespace or a UML-F library package.
	1b. The user enters the package name.
	1c. The library package is created.
Alternative Flows	—
Design Notes	—

Table 4.16: Description of UC16 – Delete library package

Use Case	UC16 – Delete library package
Actor	Pattern Developer
Description	Delete a UML-F library package and all contained patterns and tag definitions.
Preconditions	A UML-F library package with the given name exists.
Success Guarantee	The UML-F library package with the given name has been removed. All contained patterns and tag definitions, along with structure diagrams, have been removed.
Basic Flow	(Implements step 1 of the abstract use case *UC14*)
	1a. The user selects the package.
	1b. The package and its complete content is deleted.
Alternative Flows	—
Design Notes	—

Table 4.17: Description of UC17 – Create pattern definition

Use Case	UC17 – Create pattern definition
Actor	Pattern Developer
Description	Create a new UML-F pattern package.
Preconditions	There is no UML-F pattern package with an identical name in the same namespace (a UML-F library package).
Success Guarantee	A new UML-F pattern package with the given name in the selected namespace has been created.
Basic Flow	(Implements step 1 of the abstract use case *UC14*)
	1a. The user selects the namespace.
	1b. The user enters the pattern name.
	1c. The package is created.
	1d. A pattern structure diagram (class diagram) is created.
Alternative Flows	Step 1d is optional.
Design Notes	—

Table 4.18: Description of UC18 – Delete pattern definition

Use Case	UC18 – Delete pattern definition
Actor	Pattern Developer
Description	Delete a UML-F pattern package and all of its UML-F tag definitions.
Preconditions	There exists a pattern package with the given name.
Success Guarantee	The UML-F pattern package and all corresponding UML-F tag definitions have been removed. In addition, if a pattern structure diagram exists, it has been removed.
Basic Flow	(Implements step 1 of the abstract use case *UC14*)
	1a. The user selects the pattern package.
	1b. The package and all contained tag definitions are removed.
	1c. If existent, the pattern structure diagram is removed.
Alternative Flows	—
Design Notes	—

Table 4.19: Description of UC19 – Create a UML-F tag
definition

Use Case	UC19 – Create a UML-F tag definition
Actor	Pattern Developer
Description	Create a new UML-F tag definition.
Preconditions	There is no tag with an identical name in the same namespace.
Success Guarantee	A new tag definition with the given name in the selected namespace has been created.
Basic Flow	(Implements step 1 of the abstract use case *UC14*)
	1a. The user selects the namespace (a UML-F library package or a UML-F pattern package).
	1b. The user enters the tag name.
	1c. The user enters the tag applicability, e.g. class, operation, or association.
	1d. The user enters the expansion tag(s).
	1e. The tag definition is created.
	1f. The user adds the tag definition to the pattern structure diagram and models the corresponding generalizations, realizations and dependencies.
Alternative Flows	Step 1f is optional.
Design Notes	—

Table 4.20: Description of UC20 – Delete a UML-F tag
definition

Use Case	UC20 – Delete a UML-F tag definition
Actor	Pattern Developer
Description	Delete a UML-F tag definition.
Preconditions	There exists a UML-F tag with the given name.
Success Guarantee	The UML-F tag has been deleted.
Basic Flow	(Implements step 1 of the abstract use case *UC14*)
	1a. The user selects the tag definition.
	1b. The tag definition is removed from the model.
Alternative Flows	—

Table 4.20: Descr. of UC20 – Delete a UML-F tag definition (cont.)

Design Notes	—

4.2 Nonfunctional Requirements

In this section nonfunctional requirements for PANEX are described. Nonfunctional requirements are for the most part tied to quality attributes [Azu04, LCLRC03]. In the IEEE Guide to the Software Engineering Body of Knowledge, nonfunctional requirements are defined as *"the ones that act to constrain the solution. Nonfunctional requirements are sometimes known as constraints or quality requirements. They can be further classified according to whether they are performance requirements, maintainability requirements, safety requirements, reliability requirements, or one of many other types of software requirement"* [SWE04, chapter 2.1.3].

To identify all relevant nonfunctional requirements, it is best practice to use predefined lists of nonfunctional requirements and check the project's needs against them. This helps to improve the consistency of the requirements, their completeness, and their unambiguity. According to Firesmith, many requirements documents lack in these attributes [Fir03].

For the PANEX project, the standard quality model for software systems as specified in the ISO/IEC standard 9126-1 [ISO01] was used to identify the nonfunctional requirements. The quality requirements for a prototypical tool obviously are by far less stringent than they are for a commercial software product. Nevertheless, it is important to specify them explicit.

In the next section 4.2.1, the industry standard quality model for software systems is presented. The subsequent sections 4.2.2 to 4.2.7 then state the nonfunctional requirements for the PANEX tool by following the structure proposed in the quality model specification. Only requirements that have been identified as essential for the tool implementation are specified.

4.2.1 The ISO/IEC 9126-1 Quality Model

In the software engineering community, many approaches dealing with software requirements and software quality are known [BBF+02]. One approach that deals with the quality of software products is the ISO/IEC standard 9126-1 [ISO01]. This standard defines a quality model in terms of *internal quality*, *external quality*, and *quality in use*. The model can be used to evaluate the overall quality, but also certain quality-related aspects of a software product. *Internal quality* is evaluated using the software product's internal attributes, and *external quality* is evaluated at runtime. The user's point of view of the software quality in a certain environmental context is captured in the *quality in use*.

For the external and internal quality, the standard defines six characteristics [ISO01]:

1. Functionality: The capability of the software product to provide functions which meet stated and implied needs when the software is used under specified conditions.

2. Reliability: The capability of the software product to maintain a specified level of performance when used under specified conditions.

3. Usability: The capability of the software product to be understood, learned, used and attractive to the user, when used under specified conditions.

4. Efficiency: The capability of the software product to provide appropriate performance, relative to the amount of resources used, under stated conditions.

5. Maintainability: The capability of the software product to be modified. Modifications may include corrections, improvements, or adaptation of the software to changes in environment, and in requirements and functional specifications.

6. Portability: The capability of the software product to be transferred from one environment to another.

Each characteristic is further subdivided into subcharacteristics. Table 4.21 shows the characterization for internal and external quality, as proposed in the ISO/IEC 9126-1 standard, along with a short definition for every subcharacteristic. The table is adopted from the paper of Botella et al. [BBF+02] and from the lecture notes of Chamillard [Cha05].

Table 4.21: ISO/IEC 9126-1 quality attributes

Charact.	Subcharact.	Short definition
Functionality	Suitability	Presence and appropriateness of a set of functions for specified tasks.
	Accuracy	Provision of right or agreed results or effects.
	Interoperability	Ability to interact with specified systems.
	Security	Prevention of unauthorized access to data.
	Compliance	Adherence to application related standards or conventions.

Table 4.21: ISO/IEC 9126-1 quality attributes (cont.)

Charact.	Subcharact.	Short definition
Reliability	Maturity	Frequency of failure by faults in the software.
	Fault tolerance	Ability to keep a given level of performance in case of faults.
	Recoverability	Capability to reestablish a certain level of performance after faults.
	Compliance	Adherence to reliability related standards or conventions.
Usability	Understandability	Users' effort for recognizing software structure and applicability.
	Learnability	Users' effort for learning software application.
	Operability	Users' effort for operation and operation control.
	Attactiveness	Capability to be attractive to the user.
	Compliance	Adherence to usability related standards or conventions.
Efficiency	Time behavior	Response, processing times, and throughput rates.
	Resource behavior	Amount of resources used and the duration of such use.
	Compliance	Adherence to efficiency related standards or conventions.
Maintain-ability	Analysability	Identification of deficiencies, failure causes, parts to be modified, etc.
	Changeability	Effort needed for modification, fault removal, or environmental change.
	Stability	Risk of unexpected effects of modifications.
	Testability	Effort needed for validating the modified software.
	Compliance	Adherence to maintainability related standards or conventions.
Portability	Adaptability	Opportunity for adaptation to different environments.
	Installability	Effort needed to install the software in a given environment.
	Co-existence	Capability to co-exist with other independent software in a common environment.
	Replacability	Opportunity and effort of using software replacing other.

Table 4.21: ISO/IEC 9126-1 quality attributes (cont.)

Charact.	Subcharact.	Short definition
	Compliance	Adherence to conventions and standards related to portability.

4.2.2 Functionality Requirements

Interoperability: The PANEX tool shall be able to integrate seamless into the CASE tool. Since PANEX and the CASE tool both operate on the same data, their functionality shall be complementary, i.e. there shall be no duplication of functionality, and their user interface shall work in a consistent manner.

Compliance: The model data generated has to be compatible with the CASE tool's standard. This implies that the underlying metamodel can not be changed by PANEX and that the model data has to be readable by the CASE tool even in the absence of the PANEX extension.

4.2.3 Reliability Requirements

Due to the fact that the PANEX tool is a prototypical implementation of a software tool supporting the UML-F profile for framework architectures, no quality criteria regarding reliability have to be met.

4.2.4 Usability Requirements

Learnability: It is sufficient for the PANEX tool to support English as user interface language, even if localization is supported by the underlying CASE tool. The tool implementation shall provide a consistent and easy to handle user interface, including menus and commands, throughout the whole application to assist new users getting familiar with the tool. In addition, the focus shall be on understandable messages and simple user interaction concepts, such as dialogs and wizard interfaces.

Operability: Acceptance of a CASE tool to a large part depends on how efficient and easy it can be used in real-world situations. For the PANEX tool, the functionality required by the application user (cf. section 4.1.2 on page 76), and in particular the functionality required by the framework developer (cf. section 4.1.3 on page 77) are essential. Thus, these functions shall be implemented such that they can be performed with as little user interaction as possible, maintaining the simple user interface requirement.

Compliance: The PANEX user interface shall seamlessly integrate into the user interface paradigm used by the underlying CASE tool, to provide a consistent interface and to keep the learning curve flat.

4.2.5   Efficiency Requirements

Compliance: The PANEX tool implementation has to adhere to the efficiency policy used by the underlying CASE tool.

4.2.6   Maintainability Requirements

Changeability: Due to the prototypical nature of the project, it has to be designed and implemented with regard to changes of functional requirements and also of nonfunctional requirements.

Testability: The implementation has to allow for easy testing of partial functionality. Moreover, it must deliver test interfaces and provide a set of unit tests that covers the basic functionality. The usage of an established unit test framework is desirable.

Compliance: Testability support by the PANEX tool shall adhere to the standards used by the underlying CASE tool. If these are not sufficient to deliver the degree of testability needed, the methods used to improve the product's testability have to be compliant to the CASE tool's standards.

4.2.7   Portability Requirements

Installability: The PANEX tool shall be realized as a separate software component that can be loaded by the underlying CASE tool on demand. Thus, the PANEX tool extension has to be implemented using the CASE tool's plug-in architecture. Most likely, this results in a straight-forward installation procedure, provided that a running copy of the CASE tool is already installed on the target system.

Co-existence: The PANEX plug-in has to be able to co-exist with other plug-ins loaded by the underlying CASE tool without causing side effects.

Compliance: Although restricted by the underlying CASE tool, portability is an important issue for the project. Thus, the PANEX implementation should not further restrict the portability provided by the CASE tool.

CHAPTER 5

CASE Tool Selection

Selecting the underlying CASE tool is a critical step for the realization of the PANEX tool vision. A carefully chosen base system is an important foundation for the tool's construction. Any obstacle that stems from limitations of the CASE tool hinders the development process. In the worst case, the fact that it is not possible to realize one of the must-have features presented in section 3.2, will be noticed even after the implementation phase has already started.

Due to the growing complexity of software tool environments, it is difficult evaluate available tools on whether they are suitable for a certain application context. For that reason, it is important to specify a set of well-defined evaluation criteria. This prevents the evaluating person from getting lost in some tool details, while trying to get an overall impression of the tool's basic capabilities.

This chapter presents the CASE tool that builds the foundation of the PANEX tool, and the rationale for the tool selection. In the first section, the criteria for the selection of the CASE tool are defined, and four different CASE tools are evaluated against these criteria. The second section presents the rationale for the decision for one particular CASE tool. In the last section, the tool's basic concepts regarding to UML compliance, user interface paradigm, and software architecture are presented.

5.1   Tool Evaluation

This section presents the evaluation of the CASE tools. First, criteria are defined for the evaluation process. Then four CASE tools are evaluated, two commercial products from the market leading producer of CASE tools, and two open-source implementations.

5.1.1   Evaluation Criteria

The realizability of user requirements, i.e. the must-have features specified in section 3.2, is the most important criterion for the selection of a CASE tool. If this criterion is satisfied by several tools, further attributes have to be evaluated in order to come to a reasonable decision. These attributes are partly derived from the nonfunctional requirements described in section 4.2 on page 91. The following criteria are used:[1]

I. **Visualization of UML-F tags** (1): Means the realizability of the feature defined in section 3.2.1 on page 66. The ideal tool would support all three visualization approaches: *UML-F stereotypes*, *Pattern mapping notation*, and *Pattern marker notation*.

II. **Support of tag groups** (2): Means the realizability of the feature defined in section 3.2.2 on page 69.

III. **Moving between layers** (2): Means the realizability of the feature defined in section 3.2.3 on page 69.

IV. **Pattern annotation procedure** (2): Means the realizability of the feature defined in section 3.2.4 on page 70.

V. **Support for domain specific patterns** (2): Means the realizability of the feature defined in section 3.2.5 on page 70.

VI. **UML Compliance** (3): Means the UML version the tool is compliant to.

VII. **Usability** (3): Means the tool's usability for users at the beginner as well as at the advanced level.

VIII. **Open Standards** (4): Means whether the tool is compliant to open standards, such as *XML Metadata Interchange (XMI)*.

IX. **Portability** (4): Means the operating system platforms that are supported.

---

[1]The subscript number in parentheses denotes the criterion's significance. For instance, *(1)* denotes a criterion with highest significance, and *(4)* a criterion with least significance.

5.1.2 Rational Rose 2003

The first product for evaluation is *Rational Rose 2003* by *IBM Corporation*. This commercial product claims to be the market leader of the UML modeling tool market. The large market share certainly is a plus in the overall evaluation of the tool. Rose 2003 is available in several different versions, making it suitable for application domains such as software architecture design, database design, round-trip engineering, and real-time systems design.

For the purpose of evaluating the most important criteria (I to V), the power of the plug-in interface is the main aspect to look at. Rose 2003 provides the plug-in interface *Rose Extensibility Interface* (*REI*) for modules written in a proprietary scripting language. The language provides a query interface to access model elements and allows for their manipulation. It is possible create user interface elements such as dialogs. The whole set of REI interfaces also is available to external programs via COM interfaces. As it is not possible to influence the visualization of model elements in a diagram, this tool fails to meet the most important criterion (I). There is no built-in support for design patterns.

Rational Rose in the version 2003 supports the complete set of UML 1.4 diagrams. Interoperability is provided by a model import- and export interface that supports XMI 1.3.

On the usability sector, the product's user interface is very powerful and intuitive. A plus is the maturity and efficiency of the user interaction concepts, e.g. dialog-free creation of new model elements.

Rose 2003 is available on a variety of platforms, including several Windows versions, all major UNIX derivatives, and LINUX. It also supports a wide variety of programming languages, including Ada, C++, C# and Java.

Further information is available at the product website [Rat05].

5.1.3 Rational Rose XDE

The second commercial product, also from *IBM Corporation*, is called *Rational Rose XDE*. XDE is a new product, independent of the Rational Rose product line. It integrates seamlessly into the *Eclipse* development environment. The main application domain of XDE is round-trip engineering, including coding assistance.

XDE provides two plug-in interfaces that can be accessed by Windows applications via COM or by Java applications using the provided Java-COM bridge. The *Rational XDE Extensibility* (*RXE*) interface provides a query interface for model elements, but write access is not allowed. Furthermore, access to the user interface is rather restricted. The second interface, *Rational*

XDE Developer SDK (*XDK*), is a more sophisticated interface that allows for full access to all model elements. Due to the fact that XDE is integrated in the Eclipse environment, any user interface implemented as Eclipse plug-in can access the whole model using the XDK interface. The product also supports design patterns and it is possible to define custom pattern asset specifications. The pattern engine's wizard is customizable. It fires events on user actions that can be processed using Java scripts, Java classes or C# classes. Furthermore, a so-called *Menu-Extender* is available that can be used to define custom menus in the XDE environment. Thus, XDE passes criteria *II* to *V*. Unfortunately, it is not supported to influence the visualization of model elements in a diagram. For that reason it fails in the most important evaluation criterion *I*.

Rational Rose XDE supports UML 1.4, and as interchange format XMI 1.3. The user interface is similar to Rose 2003, but somewhat easier to handle. A drawback of the tool is its rather restricted platform support, as XDE runs on Windows systems only. The supported programming languages are Java and C#.

Further information is available at the product website [Rat05].

5.1.4 Fujaba Tool Suite

Fujaba, an open source tool, is the third tool for evaluation. *"The primary topic of the Fujaba Tool Suite project is to provide an easy to extend UML and Java development platform with the ability to add plug-ins"*, as stated on the tool's website [Fuj05]. Fujaba is developed at the University of Paderborn and is available under the terms of the GPL license.

The tool's implementation language is Java and the plug-in interface accepts Java components. The plug-in architecture is mature and powerful. Full access to model elements is available as well as customization of the user interface. It is also possible to add new diagram types in form of plug-ins. Thus, Fujaba passes in all the mandatory evaluation criteria *I* to *V*.

The UML standard supported by Fujaba is 1.3, but not all diagrams are supported. By default, only class diagrams, activity diagrams, and state chart diagrams are enabled. The tool uses a proprietary storage format, but import and export tools supporting XMI 1.1 are available.

A shortcoming of Fujaba is its user interface. The navigation is not comfortable and the features provided for structuring the model are insufficient for large models. For instance, diagrams can not be placed in package hierarchies.

Due to the fact that Fujaba is implemented in Java without any dependencies to a certain operating system, it can be run on any platform providing a JVM. Java also is the programming language supported for reverse engineering.

5.1.5   ArgoUML

ArgoUML is an open source tool that originated as a research project at the University of California, Irvine, and now is developed by the open source community. It is available for free without any license restrictions [Arg05a].

The tool is a pure Java implementation. The plug-in interface, which is quite powerful, accepts Java components to extend the tool. Full access to the model elements is available through interfaces that are structured according to the UML 1.3 metamodel. The user interface can be extended by plug-ins, and Menus, diagrams, and property panels can be added to the tool. Also reverse engineering plug-ins for arbitrary programming languages can be realized. Thus, ArgoUML passes all the mandatory evaluation criteria *I* to *V*.

ArgoUML's metamodel is fully compliant to UML 1.3, and the tool supports all diagrams. In the most recent versions 0.16 to 0.18, however, sequence diagrams are disabled by default due to technical problems. XMI files in version 1.0 are used as the main storage format for the model, and a proprietary format is used for diagram persistence.

The user interface ArgoUML provides is comfortable. The arrangement of model elements is clear, intuitive, and completely customizable. A highlight is the so-called *critics* subsystem, which is a customizable set of guidelines and recommendations that are permanently checked against the model. Discrepancies are reported to the user in a non-intrusive manner.

Due to the fact that ArgoUML is a pure Java implementation, it can be run on any platform providing a JVM. A whole set of programming language plug-ins are available from the website, including C++, C#, IDL ,Java and PHP. ArgoUML uses JUnit [JUn05] throughout the whole implementation to ensure correctness.

5.1.6   Other CASE Tools

Several other CASE tools have been evaluated to find the most suitable base system for the implementation of PANEX. As these tools have very limited extensibility features, they have not been evaluated in detail. These tools are *Ameos*, *Objecteering*, *ObjectiF*, *OTW*, and *Together*.

5.2 And the Winner is ... ArgoUML

Table 5.1 shows the results of the evaluation presented in the previous section:

Table 5.1: CASE tool evaluation matrix

Criterion	Priority	Rose 2003	Rose XDE	Fujaba	ArgoUML
I	(1)	×	×	√	√
II	(2)	?	√	√	√
III	(2)	?	√	√	√
IV	(2)	?	√	√	√
V	(2)	?	√	√	√
VI	(3)	1.4	1.4	1.3	1.3
VII	(3)	+	+	−	○
VIII	(4)	○	○	○	+
IX	(4)	Linux, Unix, Windows	Windows	Java	Java

Key:	√ ... realizable × ... not realizable ? ... realizability uncertain
	+ ... positive assessment ○ ... neutral − ... negative assessment
	(1) ... highest priority (4) ... lowest priority

It is easy to see that, according to the specified evaluation criteria, *ArgoUML* is the best choice
as base system for the implementation of PANEX.

5.3 Introduction to ArgoUML

This section gives a brief introduction to ArgoUML and its software architecture. The full
documentation for both, the tool user and the developer, can be found on the project website
[Arg05a].

ArgoUML (originally named *Argo/UML*) started as a research project at the University of
California, Irvine, and was intentionally planned to be an experimentation system for cogni-
tive support features in CASE tools [Rob99]. After the tool has been made available to the
public domain as open source project in February 1999, a growing community of researchers,
UML users, and open source enthusiasts contributed to the project. Since then, extensions to
ArgoUML have been subject to various research projects [Ski01].

5.3.1   UML Compliance

One of the key goals of the ArgoUML project is to provide a tool that is fully compliant to UML version 1.3:

"The vision of ArgoUML is to provide a tool that helps people work with a UML model. The UML model might later on be used in some other tool. [...] The ambition is to implement all of UML. This means that no matter how you use UML, ArgoUML will always be a working tool." [Arg05b, section 3.2]

Due to technical problems in the implementation of sequence diagrams, the principal developers decided to disable this diagram type in the most recent versions 0.16 to 0.18.

5.3.2   User Interface

Figure 5.1 shows the main window layout of a typical ArgoUML session.

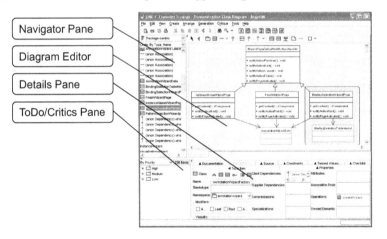

Figure 5.1: ArgoUML window layout

Besides standard user interface components such as a menu bar, a tool bar, and a status bar, the ArgoUML window comprises the following components:

Navigator Pane: The *Navigator*, also called *Explorer*, shows a tree view of the model elements and is used to navigate in the model. The navigation tree can be customized to several layout formats: *Package-centric*, *Class-centric*, *Diagram-centric*, *Inheritance-centric*, *Class associations*, *State-centric*, and *Transition-centric*.

Diagram Editor: The active diagram is shown in the *diagram editor* and can be modified there. It contains a separate tool bar providing convenient access to all modeling tools available for the active diagram type.

Details Pane: The details pane shows all properties of the model element selected in the *navigator* or in the *diagram editor* and provides a convenient way of changing them. The properties shown include UML model properties, such as name, cardinality, and visibility, but also layout related properties such as color and font. In addition, code generation settings for the model element are shown in this pane.

ToDo/Critics Pane: This pane contains messages generated from the *Critics subsystem*. In addition, this pane contains *To-do items* defined by the tool user.

5.3.3   ArgoUML Architecture

The ArgoUML system is split into subsystems with clearly defined responsibilities[2] [Arg05b, chapter 4]. Every subsystem resides in its own Java package. The subsystems are organized in layers: *Low-level subsystems*, *Model subsystems*, *View and Control subsystems* and *Loadable subsystems*.

Low-level Subsystems

Three low-level subsystems provide infrastructure services to subsystems on higher layers: *Logging*, *Internationalization (i18n)* and *JRE with utils*.

Model Subsystems

ArgoUML's architecture includes four model subsystems, residing on the second lowest subsystem layer:

1. The *Model subsystem* provides a modifiable storage for UML model elements and diagrams. It consists of a complete set of methods to create, modify, store, load and

---

[2]At the time of writing this book, the subsystem splitting has not jet been completed. ArgoUML is a continually developed open source product, and the development community is very active. Since PANEX already benefits from the subsystem architecture, it is discussed in this section.

examine the model and to register listeners for changes of model element properties. Several factory and helper interfaces are defined to ensure independence of the underlying persistence framework.[3]

2. To-do items are managed by the *To-do items subsystem*. It is responsible for their creation, deletion and persistence.

3. The *GUI Framework subsystem* provides an infrastructure with menus, tabs and panes available to the other subsystems to fill with actions and contents. Currently, this functionality for the most part is provided by the GEF library, which is discussed in section 5.3.5 on page 107.

4. The *Help system* provides the menu actions that invoke the help and other documentation. At present, this subsystem is not yet implemented.

View and Control Subsystems

Seven high-level subsystems form the *View and Control subsystems* level:

1. A graphical view of the diagrams in the model is generated by the *Diagram subsystem*. Model elements shown in diagrams are modifiable. This subsystem depends on the Model subsystem as well as on the GUI Framework subsystem.

2. The *Property panels subsystem* provides a form view of the diagrams and the model elements. It depends on the Model subsystem and on the GUI Framework subsystem.

3. The *Navigator* or *Explorer subsystem* provides tree views of the model elements, diagrams and other objects. This subsystem depends on the Model subsystem and on the GUI Framework subsystem.

4. The *Code Generation subsystem* provides common code and a management entity, where each programming language plug-in with code generation capabilities has to register. Dependency: *Model subsystem*.

5. The *Reverse Engineering subsystem* provides a management entity where programming language plug-ins that implement reverse engineering functionality have to register. In addition, common reverse engineering functions for all programming languages are supported.
Dependency: *Model subsystem*.

---

[3]Currently, the model subsystem internally uses the NSUML library [NSU05] to implement the UML metamodel and for model persistence. But since this library only supports the UML 1.3 metamodel, the change to another metamodel framework is already scheduled in the project road-map.

6. Mechanisms to load and to unload auxiliary plug-in modules are provided by the *Module loader*. It is not dependent on any of the *model* or *view and control subsystems*.

7. The *Application subsystem* provides the entry point for launching the ArgoUML application. Its responsibility is to start up the tool environment. It is dependent on the following subsystems: *Module loader subsystem, Diagram subsystem, Property panels subsystem, Explorer subsystem* and *To-do items subsystem*.

Loadable Subsystems

Several features of ArgoUML are implemented as *loadable subsystems* to allow for an easy customization of the tool environment. This kind of loadable modules includes programming language plug-ins, critics and checklist plug-ins, and the OCL plug-in.

5.3.4   Plug-In Interface

ArgoUML supports several different types of plug-ins. Every plug-in has to implement a certain interface that specifies the required operations.

The interface ArgoModule specifies general operations for a loadable module, such as operations for initialization and shutdown, and for requesting module information like name, author, version, and description.

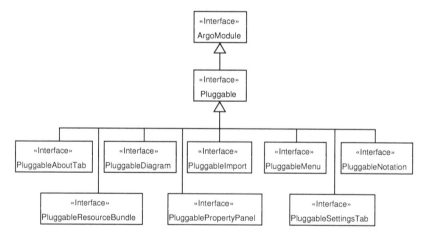

Figure 5.2: ArgoUML Plug-In interfaces

Plug-ins are loadable modules that are replacements or additions to standard ArgoUML functionality. They have to implement one of the subinterfaces of Pluggable, which defines an interface for querying a plug-in's context sensitive enabled status, i.e. *enabled* or *disabled*. Figure 5.2 on the facing page shows the hierarchy of ArgoUML plug-in interfaces.

The *Module loader* is responsible for loading plug-ins. Loadable modules generally are packaged in .jar files. There are several places where the plug-ins to be loaded can be specified. First, the module loader searches the *CLASSPATH* for any modules to load. Then several locations are searched for configuration files:[4]

```
$ARGO_HOME$\.argo.modules
$ARGO_HOME$\argo.modules
$USER_HOME$\.argo.modules
$USER_HOME$\argo.modules
$JAVA_HOME$\jre\lib\.argo.modules
$JAVA_HOME$\jre\lib\argo.modules
```

The *Application subsystem* keeps track of all loaded plug-ins and notifies them in case any context information has changed, e.g. a model element was selected in the active diagram or a model element's name has changed.

Once loaded, a plug-in has access to all public ArgoUML classes.

5.3.5   GEF – Graphical Editor Framework

The *Graphical Editor Framework* (*GEF*) provides the basic infrastructure needed by ArgoUML to build a user interface capable of visualizing and manipulating graph-based models. In addition, GEF provides a persistence mechanism for the layout of diagrams. ArgoUML uses this persistence mechanism to store its diagrams.

GEF is an abstract implementation of a graphical editor. In other words, the framework does not need to know anything about the underlying graph model. It is based on the *Model-View-Controller* pattern [BMR+96].

Three building blocks of a graph are distinguished: *Nodes* are the main entities represented as figures in a diagram. They may comprise several *ports*. Ports can be represented as separate figures. *Edges* connect nodes through their ports. Figure 5.3 on the next page shows an example of an edge connecting two nodes through their ports.

---

[4]$ARGO_HOME$ refers to ArgoUML's installation directory, $USER_HOME$ refers to the current user's home directory and $JAVA_HOME$ denotes the JDK installation directory.

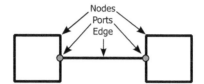

Figure 5.3: GEF graph model

Seven major concepts are essential in the editor framework:

Figure: A *fig* (short for *figure*) is a primitive shape. This can be, for instance, a circle, a cube, or some text, but also a line or an arrowhead. Figures are the diagram elements visible to the user.

Layer: A *layer* contains figs that are ordered from back to front.

Diagram: A *diagram* consists of a *LayerPerspective* and a tool bar. A LayerPerspective is a layer whose model is a connected graph.

Selection: *Selections* keep track of the selected diagram items. In addition, they might have certain effects on the selected items, such as resizing or rotating them.

Command: A *cmd* (short for *command*) performs an action on the selected or on all diagram items. For example, CmdDeleteFromModel removes the selected diagram items from the underlying model. Also actions that are related to the whole application, like CmdSave or CmdExit, are implemented as commands.

Mode: Visual editing is supported by *modes*. They process user input events and execute commands on the affected figs. For instance, *ModeCreate* creates a new figure at the position the user selects in the diagram.

Editor: The *editor* stores the data needed for the current editing session, e.g. the current *mode*. It also acts as *mediator* (cf. [GHJV95]) for all other parts and thus is responsible for message routing. The editor can contain several *layers*.

The graphical editor framework is developed as an independent open-source project [GEF05] and is used in several applications other than CASE tools.

CHAPTER 6

PANEX Software Design

"Mission defines strategy, after all, and strategy defines structure."
(Peter F. Drucker)

Although the chapter's opening quote from the prominent management authority in its original context is about business management [Dru01, p. 72], it perfectly describes the approach employed for the design of the PANEX tool. The *mission* is to bring together the requirements for the tool implementation of the UML-F approach as described in chapter 4 and the CASE tool chosen as basis for the implementation, as described in chapter 5. Since ArgoUML, as any other CASE tool, has some restrictions on the extensibility and some peculiarities in handling certain things, a *strategy* capable of solving these problems has to be found. Once the strategy is clear, the software *structure* has to be defined. Clearly, the ArgoUML framework enforces a certain architecture on its plug-ins and the freedom to structure a solution is rather restricted. Nevertheless, the size of the PANEX implementation demands for the explicit design of an appropriate software architecture.

6.1   Realization Problem Areas

The next step towards the completion of the mission – implementing the requirements defined in chapter 4 in a plug-in for ArgoUML – is to identify potential problem areas where the

ArgoUML framework may be too restricted to support the needed functionality from scratch, and to find solutions for these problems. This section describes these problem areas along with their solution.

6.1.1   User Interaction

An area where ArgoUML might cause problems is the user interaction paradigm. ArgoUML's user interface, as shown in figure 5.1 on page 103, is based on panes that allows direct user input to navigate in the *explorer*, and to directly manipulate model element properties in the *details pane*. Thus, dialogs are not used very often.

PANEX has to implement user interface elements to navigate through the UML-F library, through pattern instances, and through the expansion hierarchy of the patterns defined. A tree-like visualization seems to be the best-suited alternative (see tables 4.1, 4.2 on page 80 and table 4.6 on page 83). The straightforward solution would be a multi-tab explorer, such that the user could switch between model and UML-F navigation.

Unfortunately, the explorer pane, and also the editor pane, are not able to manage several tabs. Thus, another approach has to be employed, such as a user interface based on dialogs and wizards that are invoked through menu items. Although this approach is not consistent with the ArgoUML philosophy, it offers the possibility to build whatever user interface components are needed, whether they are supported by the underlying framework or not. Moreover, wizards that guide users simplify the interaction necessary for complex actions, such as creating a pattern instance.

6.1.2   The PANEX Pattern Engine

This section describes the heart of PANEX – the *pattern engine* – that resolves several issues coming along with the ArgoUML tool base. The pattern engine is responsible for supporting the full UML-F profile including domain specific patterns, management of pattern instances, and creation of pattern instance visualizations.

UML-F Profile Support

ArgoUML has some shortcomings in the support for the UML-F profile implementation:

- Currently, only UML version 1.3 is supported, whereas the UML profile for framework architectures, as defined in section 2.2, is a UML 2.0 profile.

- There is no support for profiles.

- Model elements can have only one stereotype.

To overcome these limitations, the solution is to use both, stereotypes and tagged values. Stereotypes and tagged values are used to define *UML-F library packages*, *UML-F pattern definitions* and *UML-F tags*. Furthermore, tagged values are used to define the UML-F tag properties *applies to* and *extension* (see section 2.2.4).

Table 6.1 lists the stereotypes that are used to define the UML-F library structure.

Table 6.1: PANEX Stereotypes

Stereotype	Extends	Description
«*UML-F Library*»	Package	Declares the stereotyped package to be a *UML-F library package*. A UML-F library package has to be a root package or a package in the namespace of another UML-F library package.
«*UML-F Pattern*»	Package	Declares the stereotyped package to be a *UML-F pattern definition*. A UML-F pattern definition has to be in the namespace of a UML-F library package.
«*UML-F TagDef*»	Interface Class Operation Association	Defines a *UML-F tag*. The UML-F tag's name is the same as the name of the stereotyped model element. The stereotyped model element has to be in the namespace of a UML-F library package or of a UML-F pattern package.

Table 6.2 on the following page lists the tagged values used to define UML-F tags and to define UML-F tag- and UML-F pattern properties.

Table 6.2: PANEX Tagged values

Tag	Applies to	Description
UML-F TagDef	Interface Class Operation Association	Defines a *UML-F tag*. The format of the tagged value is a comma separated string defining the UML-F tag's names. The tagged model element has to be in the namespace of a UML-F library package or of a UML-F pattern package.
UML-F TagExpansion	UML-F TagDef	Specifies the *expansion relation* for the UML-F tag defined by the tagged model element. Its format is a comma separated list specifying the full paths of the UML-F tag definition this UML-F tag expands to. This tagged value can only be set for model elements defining a UML-F tag, either by the stereotype «*UML-F TagDef*» of by the tagged value UML-F TagDef.
UML-F TagApplication	UML-F TagDef	Specifies the model element types the UML-F tag defined by the tagged model element can be *applied to*. Its format is a comma separated list. Valid entries are: *Interface, Class, Operation, Association*. This tagged value can only be set for model elements defining a UML-F tag, either by the stereotype «*UML-F TagDef*» of by the tagged value UML-F TagDef.
UML-F StructureDiagram	UML-F Pattern	Specifies the *pattern structure diagram* for the UML-F pattern definition. This tagged value can only be set for packages stereotyped «*UML-F Pattern*».

Figure 6.1 on the next page shows an example that uses PANEX stereotypes and tagged values to define the *Hook-Object* pattern (see table 2.4 in section 2.2.7 for the original UML-F tag definitions).[1]

In the example, the UML-F library package Essential Construction Principles Layer, which exists in the namespace of the root library package UML-F Basic Library, contains the UML-F pattern

---

[1]Strictly speaking, in ArgoUML tagged values are set in the details pane (see section 5.3.2) and not by attaching notes to the model elements. However, in this example the tagged values are specified this way in order to demonstrate the basic principle of PANEX's tag definition functionality.

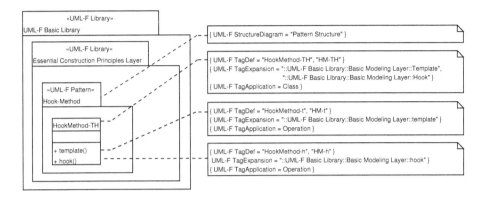

Figure 6.1: PANEX Pattern definition example

package Hook-Method. The tagged value UML-F StructureDiagram specifies that the diagram *"Pattern Structure"* in the pattern package's namespace shows the pattern structure. The pattern engine uses this diagram as template to generate pattern instance visualizations, as described below. Three UML-F tags are defined in figure 6.1:

- The tag HookMethod-TH, alias HM-TH, is defined by the tagged value UML-F TagDef in class HookMethod-TH. It expands to the two tags Template and Hook that both are defined in the library package ::UML-F Basic Library::Basic Modeling Layer. The tag can be applied to model elements of type *class* only.

- HookMethod-t, alias HM-t, is defined by the tagged value UML-F TagDef set for the template model element. ::UML-F Basic Library::Basic Modeling Layer::template is specified as the expansion tag. The HookMethod-t tag can be applied to *operations* only.

- HookMethod-h, alias HM-h, is defined by the tagged value UML-F TagDef set for the hook model element. It expands to ::UML-F Basic Library::Basic Modeling Layer::hook and can be applied to *operations* only.

Pattern Instance Management

One of the requirements for the PANEX tool is to respect the standard model format defined by the CASE tool (see section 4.2.2 on page 94). This implies that the metamodel can not be changed by PANEX.

The mapping information between model elements and pattern roles for all pattern instances, however, has to be persisted. A modified metamodel would be the easiest solution, but that would break the compatibility requirement.

The PANEX solution is to use tagged values to store the so-called *pattern binding* information. Every model element, that plays a role in at least one pattern instance, has attached the tagged value UML-F Binding. This holds the pattern binding information and is managed by the PANEX pattern engine exclusively.

The advantage – full UML compliance – comes at the cost of consistency. The existence of a pattern instance is solely indicated by a binding entry in at least one model element's UML-F Binding tag. In other words, there is no model element explicitly representing a pattern instance in the model. As a consequence, the *model event pump*, an integral part of ArgoUML that notifies subscribed listeners, such as diagram figures, about changes in the state of model elements, can not be used to guarantee consistency between model and visual representation. Thus, the PANEX tool has to make some extra efforts to overcome that problem.

PBL - The Pattern Binding Language

As described in the previous subsection, pattern binding information is stored in tagged values named UML-F Binding that are managed by PANEX. In ArgoUML only text information can be stored in tagged values. Thus, a special language, the *Pattern Binding Language*, or *PBL* for short, had to be designed as storage format for these tagged values. Listing 6.1 shows the language's EBNF description:

Listing 6.1: EBNF definition of the *PANEX Pattern Binding Language (PBL)*

```
1   # EBNF-Definition of PANEX-PBL
2   #-------------------------------------------------------------------
3   BINDINGS            ::= BINDING { ';' BINDING } .
4   BINDING             ::= '<' PATTERNINSTANCEUUID
5                           [ '|' PATTERNINSTANCENAME ]
6                           '=' TAGPATHS '>' .
7   TAGPATHS            ::= TAGPATH { ',' TAGPATH } .
8   TAGPATH             ::= '::' ELEMENTNAME  { '::' ELEMENTNAME } .
9   ELEMENTNAME         ::= NAME .
10  PATTERNINSTANCENAME ::= NAME .
11  PATTERNINSTANCEUUID ::= UUID .
12  NAME                ::= string of any characters except ':;,<>|' .
13  UUID                ::= string of any of the characters
14                          '0123456789abcdef:-' .
```

The following list describes the requirements that guided the language design and also shows the resulting language elements:

1. A model element can play roles in several pattern instances → BINDINGS, BINDING.

2. A pattern instance is represented by a unique id → PATTERNINSTANCEUUID.

3. An optional name can be specified for a pattern instance → PATTERNINSTANCENAME.

4. A model element can play several roles in a certain pattern instance → TAGPATHS.

5. Full-qualified paths are used to avoid ambiguities → TAGPATH, ELEMENTNAME.

6. Simple parsing, i.e. a *LL(1)* language → alphabet for NAME.

7. The UUIDs used by ArgoUML to identify model elements are used as unique identifiers for pattern instances → alphabet for UUID.

The following example is a simple PBL expression that indicates that the tagged model element plays the role HookMethod-TH in the pattern instance named HM Instance 1:

```
<127-0-0-1-1a23ea4:10152a369b5:-7fe6|HM Instance 1=
::UML-F Basic Library::Essential Construction Principles Layer::Hook-Method::HookMethod-TH>
```

Pattern Structure Diagrams

Two tag visualization variants are implemented in PANEX, the *pattern mapping notation* and the *pattern marker notation* (see section 3.2.1 on page 66). The problematic variant for the pattern engine is the pattern mapping notation. Figure 3.2 on page 68 shows an example of that notation: arrows from every pattern structure element to the model element playing that particular role in the pattern instance are used to indicate the pattern roles. For a user friendly visualization process, the pattern's structure has to be added automatically to the diagram to be annotated.

PANEX solves that problem by introducing so-called *pattern structure diagrams*. These diagrams serve two purposes. First, to depict the structure of a certain pattern, and second, to define the corresponding UML-F tags at the same time. An example of a pattern structure diagram is figure 6.1 on page 113, which shows the structure of the Hook-Method construction principle, but also defines the UML-F tags by setting tagged values for every model element representing a certain role of the construction principle, i.e. HookMethod-TH, template, and hook.

Pattern structure diagrams are specified by setting the tagged value UML-F StructureDiagram for the corresponding pattern package. The example figure 6.1 depicts this for the pattern package Hook-Method.

When a visualization in the pattern mapping notation is generated, PANEX automatically looks up the corresponding pattern structure diagram. Then figures representing exactly the same model elements are created in the active diagram, and their positions are set the same as they are in the original diagram, with respect to a user defined offset. Finally, the mapping arrows highlighting the pattern roles are created by the tool.

6.1.3 Graph Model Representation and Persistence

As mentioned in section 5.3.5, the GEF library uses the abstract concepts of *node*, *edge* and *port* to visualize a graph model (see figure 5.3 on page 108). This model brings several difficulties for the implementation of the two visualization variants *pattern mapping notation* and *pattern marker notation* (see section 3.2.1).

Edge-Marker Nodes

The first problem arises with the pattern mapping notation. As can be seen in figure 3.2 on page 68, arrows are used to highlight pattern roles. Unlike as shown in the figure, this visualization is not limited to class and operation roles; also association roles can be highlighted using the mapping notation. The graph model, however, does not support this feature since edges cannot own ports, and thus edges cannot be used to connect edges.

A solution for this problem is to use *PathItems*. These are figures in the graphical representation that are attached to an edge and that always stay at a certain position relative to the edge, e.g. in the middle of the edge. ArgoUML uses them, for example, to visualize cardinalities and names of associations, where text figures are used as PathItems.

PANEX uses the PathItem mechanism to attach a node, which owns a port, to both associations, the pattern instance association and the pattern structure association. This way an edge can be used to connect the two *edge-marker nodes*. Figure 6.2 on the facing page shows this situation.

One problem that comes along with this approach is that GEF's persistence mechanism is rather limited and cannot load the edge-marker nodes from a file. This is because the persistence layer cannot load a node that is a PathItem of an edge. The *mapping edge*, which connects the two edge-marker nodes, however, stores its endpoint figures. This information is preserved by the persistence layer. The endpoint figures are part of the group building the edge representation

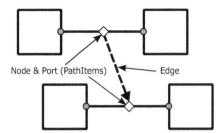

Figure 6.2: Edge-Marker-Nodes as PathItems

and thus can be used to find the corresponding edges. With that information at hand, new PathItems can be created for the edges and the mapping edges can be drawn correctly. Due to the loading order of the edges, however, it is impossible to perform this task when the mapping edge is loaded. Instead, this has to be done after all diagram elements have been loaded, which demands for the usage of the *delay-load* technique that is described below.

Pattern-Marker Groups

The graphical editor framework also introduces some problems with the implementation of the second visualization variant, the pattern marker notation. This notation uses text figures to highlight pattern roles for classes and operations (see figure 3.3 on page 68). It is required that the text figures always stay in the same position relative to the model element they belong to. For example, if the user moves a class that is annotated that way, the annotation text should follow the model element.

In PANEX, this is realized by introducing *invisible groups*, that register themselves to the annotated class and thus are notified whenever the position or the state of the class changes. This way, the group can update the positions of its members, the annotation markers, which are simple text figures provided by the framework. It is not possible to use visible groups as they are provided by GEF, since then it would not be possible to select just one of the pattern markers of a pattern instance. This is necessary, for instance, if the user wants to delete a single annotation tag, e.g. an operation marker, without affecting the other markers of the same pattern instance. Furthermore, advanced text figures also can not be used since the simple text figures GEF provides are the only ones that can store text information in the diagram layout file; this behavior is hard coded in GEF's persistence layer.

The most difficult part with this approach is, again, persistence. Since the text markers are simple text figures, they don't know the model element they belong to. In addition, due to a shortcoming in the persistence implementation, the invisible marker group looses the reference to the text markers as well as to the class figure when loaded from a file. A solution to that problem is to use invisible edges to store these references. Figure 6.3 depicts the persistence scheme for pattern markers.

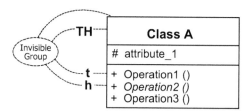

Figure 6.3: Pattern-Marker persistence scheme

Invisible edges, depicted as dashed lines, are used to store the following references:

1. From the invisible group to the annotated class.
2. From the invisible group to the pattern markers.
3. From the pattern markers to the pattern instance model elements.

Due to the fact that recovering the original references when the diagram is loaded from a file can not be performed until all diagram elements have been loaded, it is necessary to use the *delay-load* technique as described below.

Delay-Loading

As discussed in the two previous subsections, the persistence layer provided by GEF is rather limited. As a consequence, certain references needed for proper visualization are lost when a diagram is loaded from a file. These references can be recovered by using hidden elements in the diagram to overcome the GEF shortcomings. Unfortunately, recovering the references can only be done after all diagram elements have been loaded. To ensure that this prerequisite holds, a technique called *delay-loading* is used.

The term delay-loading itself illustrates the technique's nature, which is to finish the loading of specific diagram elements with a certain delay. Technically spoken, these specific diagram elements create separate threads to finish the loading work, which in our case is to recover the lost references. The threads are enqueued in the system's EventQueue using the method java.awt.EventQueue.invokeLater. When the file loading operation, which is a blocking operation, completes, these threads are activated in turn. This ensures, on one hand, that the diagram elements can be loaded at least in part and thus the loading operation terminates successfully. On the other hand, when the created threads are executed, they have access to all diagram elements needed to recover the lost references.

6.2 Use Case Implementation Plan

The result of the use case analysis represents the required functionality of PANEX, independent of the underlying CASE tool. After the problematic areas of an implementation on top of ArgoUML have been identified and appropriate solutions have been found, the next step is to try to reuse as much functionality as possible already built in the CASE tool.

This section presents the implementation plan for all use cases identified in section 4.1. First, functionality that is covered in the ArgoUML implementation is identified. Second, the remaining use cases, i.e. the ones that have to be implemented in the PANEX tool, are listed.

6.2.1 Functionality Covered by ArgoUML

Use cases that do not deal with visualization or with pattern instances are the most promising candidates for being already implemented in a CASE tool, since these two responsibilities require some extra work to be done by the UML-F tool. The functional requirements described by following use cases are covered by ArgoUML and thus do not have to be implemented in PANEX:[2]

UC5 – Delete Visualization

The user deletes the corresponding diagram figures by hand.

UC13 – Import Pattern Library

The user simply loads the ArgoUML model containing the model elements that define the UML-F library elements.

UC14 – Modify Pattern Library (abstract use case)

UC15 – Create Library Package

The user creates a package and assigns the stereotype «*UML-F Library*».

---

[2]It is interesting to note that all use cases that are associated to the pattern developer role are already covered by ArgoUML. In other words, it is not necessary to have the tool extension installed be able to build a new or to modify an existing UML-F library. Apparently, the major responsibility of PANEX is to manage pattern instances, to create visualizations and to provide a user interface for convenient navigation through the UML-F library and through the set of pattern instances.

UC16 – Delete Library Package

    The user deletes the package.

UC17 – Create Pattern Definition

    The user creates a package and assigns the stereotype «*UML-F Pattern*». In addition, a structure diagram can be specified by setting the tagged value UML-F Structure Diagram.

UC18 – Delete Pattern Definition

    The user deletes the package.

UC19 – Create UML-F Tag Definition

    The user creates a model element and assigns the stereotype «*UML-F TagDef*» or sets the tagged value UML-F TagDef. In addition, the UML-F tag's properties can be specified by setting the tagged values UML-F TagExpansion and UML-F TagApplication.

UC20 – Delete UML-F Tag Definition

    The user removes the stereotype «*UML-F TagDef*» or the tagged value UML-F TagDef from the corresponding model element.

6.2.2   PANEX Functionality

The following use cases are not covered by ArgoUML, and thus have to be implemented in the PANEX tool:

    UC1 – Browse Pattern Instances
    UC2 – Browse Pattern Expansion
    UC3 – Visualize Pattern Instance (abstract use case)
    UC4 – Create Visualization
    UC6 – Browse Pattern Library
    UC7 – Create Pattern Instance
    UC8 – Modify Pattern Instance (abstract use case)
    UC9 – Rename Pattern Instance
    UC10 – Delete Pattern Instance
    UC11 – Add UML-F Tag
    UC12 – Remove UML-F Tag

6.3 Software Design

Now, as problematic parts of the implementation have been identified, solutions have been found (section 6.1), and the amount of functionality to be built into the tool extension is specified (section 6.2), PANEX's internal architecture has to be designed.

Obviously, the solution space for the internal architecture of a plug-in is rather restricted since the framework it builds on enforces a certain architectural style. ArgoUML, for example, restricts plug-ins to conform to one of the predefined plug-in interfaces. Furthermore, an ArgoUML plug-in has to use the provided event mechanism, the model query functions, the persistence mechanism, and the user interface paradigm. Nevertheless, the size of the PANEX plug-in, originating from the variety of functions it should provide, demands for a separate design.

6.3.1 PANEX Plug-Ins

ArgoUML defines a plug-in architecture for tool extensions that can be loaded at startup. The plug-in architecture comprises a set of plug-in interfaces that declare methods specific to a plug-in's responsibilities, such as a method for creating menu items for a menu-plug-in, i.e. a plug-in that extends the ArgoUML menu. All possible plug-in interfaces are shown in figure 5.2 on page 106.

The functionality implemented by the PANEX tool extension can not be put into a single plug-in, in the sense of ArgoUML plug-in interfaces. Thus, it consists of several plug-ins. Figure 6.4 shows the class diagram of all plug-ins that are part of PANEX.

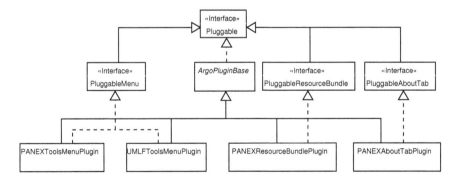

Figure 6.4: PANEX plug-Ins

ArgoPluginBase

>   This abstract base class implements the Pluggble interface, which declares methods for querying general information regarding the plug-in such as author and ArgoUML compatibility, and also the plug-in's enabled status. It is the superclass of all PANEX plug-ins.

PANEX ResourceBundlePlugin

>   This plug-in implements the PluggableResourceBundle interface and registers resources to ArgoUML that can be localized. The PANEXResourceBundlePlugin registers the strings and icons used by PANEX. By now, the language of these resources is English. The separation of the localization concern into a separate plug-in, however, eases the translation to other languages.

UMLF ToolsMenuPlugin

>   This plug-in implements the PluggableMenu interface. It provides a menu for accessing UML-F related commands. The menu is called *UML-F Tools* and is located in ArgoUML's *Tools* menu. The commands provided are:

>   - Show UML-F Library Tree
>   - Show Pattern Instances
>   - Show Pattern Expansion Tree
>   - Pattern Annotation Wizard
>   - Pattern Instance Wizard
>   - Pattern Visualization Wizard

PANEX ToolsMenuPlugin

>   This plug-in is a menu-plug-in, i.e. it implements PluggableMenu. It provides a separate menu called *PANEX Tools*, located in ArgoUML's *Tools* menu, which contains menu items for tool functions provided by PANEX. The commands provided by this menu are not related to UML-F.

PANEX AboutTabPlugin

>   Plug-ins implementing the PluggableAboutTab interface are permitted to register separate tabs in ArgoUML's *About* dialog. PANEXAboutTabPlugin registers a tab for the PANEX tool extension that shows a copyright notice.

ArgoUML looks for configuration files in certain locations (see section 5.3.4) that specify the plug-ins to be loaded by the tool. The configuration file used to load the PANEX plug-ins in ArgoUML is shown in listing 6.2 on the next page.

It is important to note that the order in which the configuration file entries appear does matter. The resource bundle plug-in has to be loaded before any other PANEX plug-in can be loaded. Unfortunately, it is not possible to define explicit dependencies between ArgoUML plug-ins, which would be a more stable solution than to rely on the order of configuration file entries.

Listing 6.2: ArgoUML configuration file for loading PANEX modules

```
1   # -----------------------------------------------------------------------
2   # Format:
3   # <module-key>=<module main class>
4   # Note: <module-key> has to be the same string as returned by the
5   #        module's getModuleKey() method (declared in interface
6   #        org.argouml.application.api.ArgoModule).
7   #        If a module is loaded through a jar-manifest, <module-key>
8   #        has to be specified in the manifest's  "Extension-name" field.
9   # -----------------------------------------------------------------------
10  #
11  module.panex.resourcebundle=  net.softwareresearch.ta.panex.argoplugin.
        PANEXResourceBundlePlugin
12  module.panex.menu.tools.umlf= net.softwareresearch.ta.panex.argoplugin.
        UMLFToolsMenuPlugin
13  module.panex.menu.tools.panex= net.softwareresearch.ta.panex.argoplugin.
        PANEXToolsMenuPlugin
14  module.panex.about= net.softwareresearch.ta.panex.argoplugin.
        PANEXAboutTabPlugin
```

6.3.2 PANEX Architecture

The PANEX architecture tries to clearly separate concerns by structuring the implementation in such a way that every concern is captured by a separate package. The package diagram in figure 6.5 on the following page shows the packages of the PANEX architecture and depicts their dependencies.

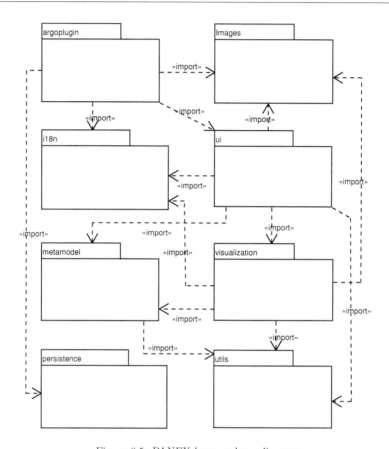

Figure 6.5: PANEX base package diagram

argoplugin

    All PANEX plug-ins (see section 6.3.1) are part of this package. Thus, this package provides the entry points for the PANEX tool extension.

Images

    This package contains the icons and images used by PANEX. The naming follows the ArgoUML convention [Arg05b].

i18n

    This package provides basic support for localized strings. All strings that appear in the user interface are defined in this package. The naming follows the convention defined in the ArgoUML developer cookbook [Arg05b].

ui   The PANEX user interface implementation resides in this package. All dialogs, wizards, and menu actions are part of the ui package.

metamodel

The UML-F profile metamodel is implemented in this package. In addition, the mechanisms necessary for the management of pattern instances are part of the metamodel package. In other words, this package is the home of the PANEX pattern engine (see section 6.1.2).

visualization

This package implements the following visualization mechanisms:

- Pattern instance visualization – pattern mapping notation
- Pattern instance visualization – pattern marker notation
- UML-F library tree model[3]
- UML-F tag expansion tree model
- Pattern instance tree model

In addition, the visualization package contains the diagram figures, which are derived from GEF classes, and which are required for both pattern instance visualization notations.

persistence

The persistence layer is implemented in this package. In fact, this just consists of a few extensions to the ArgoUML persistence layer to resolve some of its issues.

utils

This is the package where various utility classes are located.

Metamodel architecture

This subsection presents the micro-architecture of the metamodel package, which contains the implementation of the pattern engine (see section 6.1.2). Its package diagram is shown in figure 6.6 on the next page.

---

[3]All *tree models* used in PANEX conform to the interface TreeModel provided in the Swing package javax.swing.tree. They are used as model components of Swing's *Model-View-Controller* [BMR+96] based implementation of tree views in javax.swing.JTree.

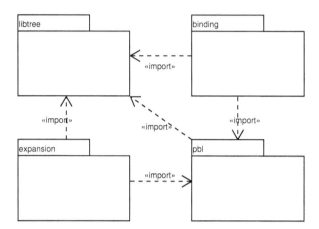

Figure 6.6: Metamodel package diagram

The metamodel package is further split into four packages:

libtree

The responsibility of this package is to model the internal class structure of a UML-F library tree. The class diagram in figure 6.7 on the facing page shows this structure.

The basic interface for all UML-F library tree elements is UMLFLibraryTreeNode. It declares the operations necessary for traversing the library tree.

The root of the tree is represented by a separate class, namely UMLFLibraryTreeRoot, that is also a tree element, i.e. it implements the UMLFLibraryTreeNode interface.

A UMLFLibraryDefinition is a tree element and represents a UML-F library package. It can contain other library packages, pattern definitions, and tag definitions. In addition, it maintains a reference to its owning tree element.

UMLFPatternDefinition is the class that models a UML-F pattern definition. It is a tree element, can contain tag definitions, and also maintains a reference to its owning tree element.

A UML-F tag definition is modeled by UMLFTagDefinition, which maintains a reference to its parent tree elements and can consist of several *sub-tag definitions*. These tag definitions are regular UML-F tag definitions, but are defined in the namespace of another tag definition. For instance, the tags template and hook in figure 6.1 on page 113 are

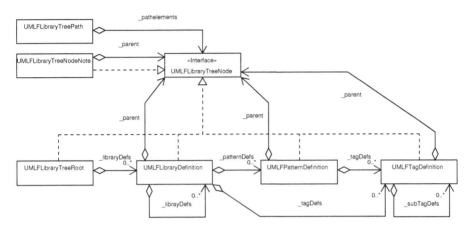

Figure 6.7: UML-F library tree class diagram

defined in the namespace of the HookMethod-TH namespace. Thus, internally these two tag definitions are represented as sub-tag definitions.

The class UMLFLibraryTreeNodeNote represents a note that can be attached to any library tree node and is used internally to enrich tree views with additional information.

Paths in the library tree are represented as distinct objects of type UMLFLibraryTreePath.

binding

This package implements the mechanism for binding model elements to pattern instances. In other words, it is responsible for the management of the UML-F Binding tagged values. Figure 6.8 on the following page shows the package's class diagram.

The package contains the factory class PatternBindingFactory. It takes configuration data (PatternBindingPatternData and PatternBindingTagData) and creates or modifies the UML-F Binding tagged values of the corresponding model elements. In addition, objects that represent the resulting pattern instance and the corresponding tag bindings (PatternInstance and TagBinding) are created.

Static utility methods, e.g. a method for renaming pattern instances, are provided by the class PatternBindingUtilities.

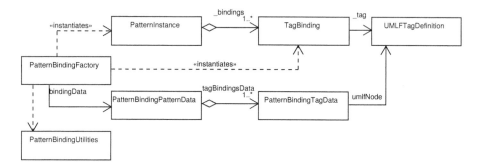

Figure 6.8: Pattern binding class diagram

expansion

The classes in the **expansion** package model the expansion relations of tags and patterns. Figure 6.9 shows the corresponding class diagram. Since pattern instances are not represented as separate model elements, a PatternExpansion is always connected to the pattern's tag expansion relations, which are modeled by the class TagExpansion. This means that a pattern expands to all the patterns its tags expand to.

The abstract class *Expansion* provides functionality common to both expansion types.

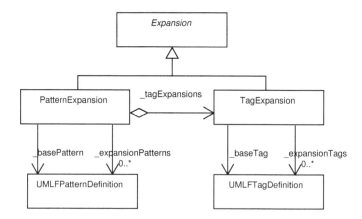

Figure 6.9: Pattern expansion class diagram

pbl

This package implements the *Pattern Binding Language (PBL)* and contains three classes. The PBLGrammar interface defines the PBL grammar, the parser for the language is implemented in PBLParser, and PBLGenerator implements a generator that can produce valid PBL expressions.

UI architecture

The micro-architecture of the ui package is discussed in this subsection. The package's responsibility is to implement dialogs, menu actions, and wizards. While the implementation of the dialogs and menu actions is not complex as thus does not demand for a separate architecture, the wizard implementation does. The main reason for this is that neither GEF nor ArgoUML provide wizard-like user interfaces, and thus the necessary infrastructure has to be built from scratch. PANEX includes a framelet[4] for building wizards: the wizframelet.

Figure 6.10 shows a package diagram that depicts the structure of the ui package.

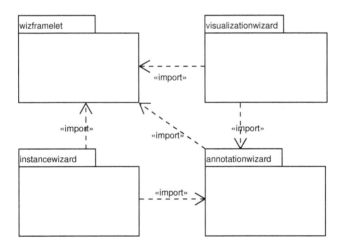

Figure 6.10: UI package diagram

All PANEX wizards use the wizard framelet, which is implemented in the wizframelet package. The annotationwizard guides the user through the task of annotating model elements and

---

[4]Refer to section 1.2.1 for the definition of the term *framelet*.

creating patter instances. The instancewizard provides a user interface for the management of pattern instances. Visualizations of pattern instances are created using the visualizationwizard. As can be seen in the package diagram, part of the former wizard's implementation is reused by the instancewizard and the visualizationwizard implementations.

Figure 6.11 depicts the class diagram for the wizard framelet.

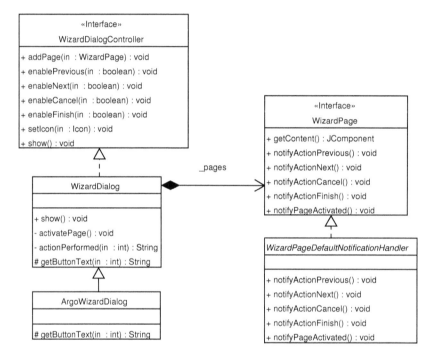

Figure 6.11: Wizframelet class diagram

The WizardDialogController interface specifies a set of methods for configuring and controlling wizards. The class WizardDialog implements this interface and provides the control logic, the page management handling, and the page notification mechanism common to all wizards. It also creates the wizard dialog and the buttons used to navigate through the wizard's pages.

ArgoWizardDialog is a class that uses ArgoUML's internationalization features to support the use of localized strings in wizards. That way WizardDialog is completely independent of ArgoUML and can be reused in other applications that have to provide functionality through wizard interfaces.

Wizards are configured by adding pages that implement the WizardPage interface. A wizard page has to provide its content in form of a JComponent. The page is notified on several events: when the page was activated, or when one of the wizard buttons for that page, i.e. *next, previous, cancel* and *finish*, was pressed. The abstract class *WizardPageDefaultNotificationHandler* provides a convenient base class for wizard pages that do not need to react on all events; all of its notification methods have an empty implementation.

Figure 6.12 shows the class diagram of the annotationwizard package.

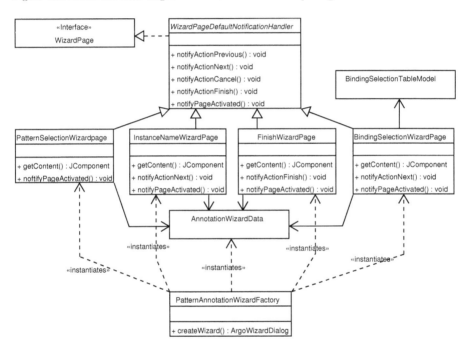

Figure 6.12: Pattern annotation wizard class diagram

The pattern annotation wizard, like all PANEX wizards, is built using the wizard framelet. The factory class PatternAnnotationWizardFactory is responsible for instantiating the wizard. First, it instantiates the wizard's pages: PatternSelectionWizardPage for the selection of a certain pattern, InstanceNameWizardPage for the specification of the pattern instance's name, BindingSelectionWizardPage for the selection of the model elements and the pattern roles they play, and FinishWizardPage that finally creates the pattern instance. Second, a new instance of ArgoWizardDialog is created and the pages are added in the order they should appear on the wizard dialog. The factory also instantiates the data object AnnotationWizardData, that is shared by all wizard pages to store the data entered by the user.

The structure of the other PANEX wizards, the pattern instance wizard in package instancewizard, and the pattern visualization wizard in package visualizationwizard, is analogous to the structure presented in figure 6.12.

Part III

PANEX at Work

Case Studies and Related Approaches

CHAPTER 7

Case Study: A Framelet for User Interface Wizards

In this chapter, a small framework in the user interface domain is used as first proof of PANEX's tool concept. This is done by depicting the user interactions necessary to appropriately document the framework. The resulting report should serve as basis for potential PANEX users to estimate the effort needed to document a certain framework.

Also a second purpose is served by the case study: The case study is presented in a *tutorial*-like style. Thus, new PANEX users may use this chapter as guide to a first annotation project in order to get familiar with the tool.

7.1 Wizard Framelet Introduction

This section gives a brief introduction to the framelet and the design patterns that have been used in the framelet's design.

The wizframelet is a small framework used for building user interfaces following the wizard-style. It is part of the PANEX implementation, and it's basic architecture is described in section 6.3.2 on page 129. The class diagram depicting the framelet structure is shown in figure 6.11 on page 130.

To be able to document the design patterns used to build the framelet, it is necessary to look at a concrete wizard application. PANEX's pattern annotation wizard is used for this purpose. Its class diagram is show in figure 6.12 on page 131.

7.1.1   Page Notification Mechanism

A special mechanism is used by the wizard framelet to notify pages whenever one of the buttons in the dialog, i.e. *next*, *previous*, *cancel*, or *finish*, was pressed, or when a certain page was activated, i.e. when it becomes the visible page. The mechanism is based on the *Hook-Object* construction principle (see section 1.1.1 on page 7). The class WizardDialog acts as the *template* class that notifies the *hook* classes. These classes are the wizard pages implementing the WizardPage interface.

7.1.2   Page Content Creation

Every wizard page is responsible for creating the content the wizard framelet shows in the dialog window. The framelet uses the *Abstract Factory* pattern (see [GHJV95, chapter 3]) to allow for a very flexible manner of creating the content objects.

The factory's *client* role is played by WizardDialog. WizardPage plays the pattern's *abstract factory* role as it specifies a common interface for all *concrete factories*, the concrete wizard pages, to create an *abstract product*. The abstract product, in the framelet context, is the class javax.swing.JComponent. The page content of any wizard page has to be a subclass of it and plays the role of a *concrete product*.

7.2   Annotating Wizframelet Patterns

This section describes the task of annotating construction principles and the design patterns. A tutorial-style approach with screen-shots is used to describe the usage of the PANEX tool. The annotation process is demonstrated by using the wizard framelet's page notification mechanism as example.

Step 1: First, after the ArgoUML tool environment has been started and the PANEX plug-ins have been loaded, it is necessary to import the predefined UML-F library. This is done by opening the file **PANEX UML-F Library Template.zargo**, which is part of the PANEX distribution. The model elements defining the UML-F library appear in the navigator pane.

It is recommended to save the project under a new name first.

Step 2: Now the framelet design can be modeled using the tools provided by ArgoUML.

Step 3: When all classes have been designed, the *Hook-Object* construction principle can be annotated.[1] This is done by starting the *pattern annotation wizard* using the menu sequence *Tools→UML-F Tools→Pattern Annotation Wizard*.

Figure 7.1 shows the wizard's first page. In this page, the UML-F library tree is shown and the pattern to be annotated has to be selected. For the example, the *Hook-Object* construction principle is selected.

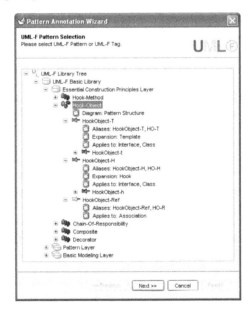

Figure 7.1: Pattern annotation wizard – Pattern selection page

---

[1]In fact, it is not mandatory to create the classes before the annotation can be performed. The pattern annotation wizard also can create new model elements.

Step 4: The next wizard page, which is show in figure 7.2, is used to enter a name for the pattern instance. Although it is not mandatory to enter a name, it is strongly recommended.

Figure 7.2: Pattern annotation wizard – Pattern instance name page

Step 5: Figure 7.3 on the next page shows the third wizard page. Here, the model elements that play roles in the pattern instance have to be selected. The table on top of the page contains a row for every pattern role and the user has to specify a model element for every role. The buttons Add tag   binding and Remove tag binding can be used to add additional rows to the table or to remove existing rows. Existing as well as new model elements can be specified using the dialog elements Create new model element or Use existing model element.

In the wizard framelet example, WizardDialog is selected as template class to be tagged as HookObject-T. Its template operation is activatePage. The hook interface is WizardPage with the hook method notifyPageActivated. The association from the template class to the hook class is specified as _pages.

Figure 7.3: Pattern annotation wizard – Model element section page

Step 6: The last wizard page summarizes the actions that will be performed in case the user presses the Finish button. Figure 7.4 shows this wizard page for the wizframlet example.

Figure 7.4: Pattern annotation wizard – Summary page

To annotate all design patterns used in the wizard framelet, the pattern annotation wizard has to be executed two more times. First, a second Hook-Object instance has to be created for the notification of button actions. Second, the Abstract Factory pattern has to be instantiated for the page content creation mechanism.

The *pattern instance browser dialog* can be used to view all pattern instances of the current model. It is opened by using the menu sequence *Tools→UML-F Tools→Show Pattern Instances*. Figure 7.5 shows the pattern instance browser dialog for the wizard framelet example after all pattern instances have been created.

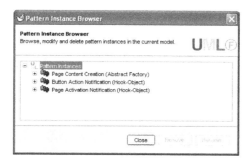

Figure 7.5: Pattern instance browser dialog

7.3   Visualizing Pattern Instances

In this section the usage of the PANEX tool for the purpose of creating pattern instance visualizations is explained. The description is organized in style of a tutorial, with screen-shots depicting the pattern visualization wizard pages. The visualization process is demonstrated by using the wizard framelet's page notification as example.

Step 1: The first step is to select the diagram where the visualization will be put by selecting it in the navigator pane.

Step 2: Next, the *pattern visualization wizard* is started using the menu sequence *Tools→UML-F Tools→Pattern Visualization Wizard*.

Figure 7.6 on the facing page shows the wizard's first page. In this page, the tree of all pattern instances is shown and the pattern instance to be visualized has to be selected. For this example, the Page Activation Notification (Hook-Object) instance is selected.

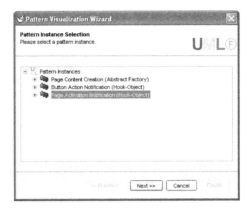

Figure 7.6: Pattern visualization wizard – Pattern instance selection page

Step 3: The next wizard page, as show in figure 7.7, is used to select the expansion layer for the visualization.

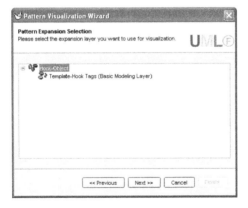

Figure 7.7: Pattern visualization wizard – Pattern expansion selection page

The expansion layer specifies which pattern in the expansion hierarchy is used for the visualization. For example, the Page Activation   Notification instance can be visualized at the Essential Construction   Principles Layer, i.e. the layer the Hook-Object construction principle resides on, or at the underlying Basic Modeling Layer, which would result in a visualization that shows basic template and hook tags.

Step 4: Page three of the visualization wizard offers the choice for the visual notation to be used. The pattern mapping notation or the pattern marker notation can be selected, which are described in detail in section 3.2.1 on page 66. Figure 7.8 shows the corresponding wizard page.

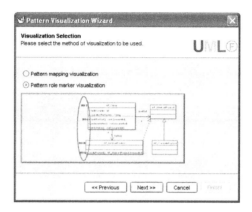

Figure 7.8: Pattern visualization wizard – Notation selection page

Step 5: The next wizard page, as shown in figure 7.9, is used to select the details to be shown in the resulting visualization. In other words, it can be selected whether class tags, operation tags, and association tags are visualized in the active diagram.

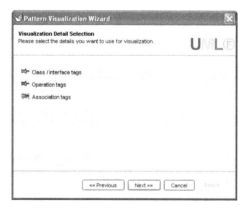

Figure 7.9: Pattern visualization wizard – Details selection page

Step 6: Figure 7.10 shows the last page of the wizard that summarizes the user's choices. When the user presses the Finish button, the visualization will be generated.

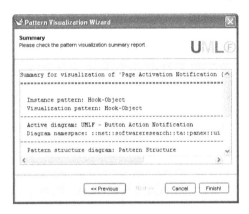

Figure 7.10: Pattern visualization wizard – Summary page

In case the user chooses the pattern mapping notation, the location where the pattern structure in the active diagram will be put has to be specified, i.e. the user clicks on the target location. Figure 7.11 shows the resulting class diagram for the Page Activation Notification pattern instance. Note that the diagram elements shown in this figure have been rearranged manually to reduce the overlapping of pattern mapping arrows and model element figures.

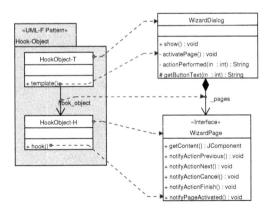

Figure 7.11: Page activation class diagram – Pattern mapping notation

When the pattern marker notation is chosen by the user, the marker figures are placed automatically next to the corresponding model element figures in the active diagram. The result for the Page Activation Notification pattern instance is shown in figure 7.12.

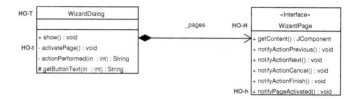

Figure 7.12: Page activation class diagram – Pattern marker notation

Figure 7.13 shows the annotated class diagram for the Button Action Notification instance of the Hook-Object construction principle using the pattern mapping notation.

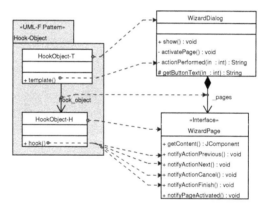

Figure 7.13: Button notification class diagram – Pattern mapping notation

In figure 7.14 on the next page the same class diagram is shown, but annotated using the pattern marker notation and at a different pattern expansion layer (the Basic Modeling Layer).

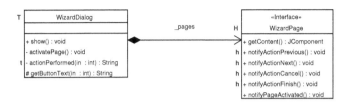

Figure 7.14: Button notification class diagram – Pattern marker notation

The annotated class diagram for the third pattern instance defined for the wizard framelet, the Page Content Creation instance of the Abstract Factory pattern, is shown in figure 7.15. Note that the class InstanceNameWizardPage is not part of the framework itself. It is part of the *pattern annotation wizard* and is representative for all other wizard pages, which also play the *Concrete Factory* role in the pattern instance.

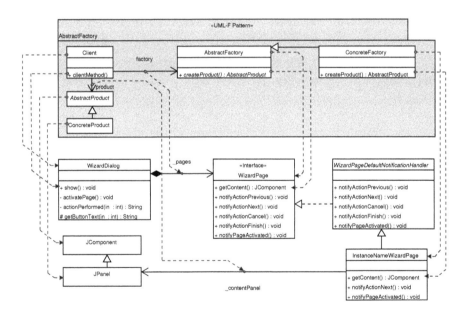

Figure 7.15: Page content creation class diagram – Pattern mapping notation

The pattern marker notation for that pattern instance is shown in figure 7.16 on the next page.

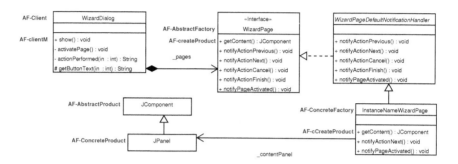

Figure 7.16: Page content creation class diagram – Pattern marker notation

7.4 Modifying Pattern Instances

A functionality regularly used in the everyday work with the PANEX system is the modification of pattern instances. In the wizframelet case study, for example, the Abstract Factory pattern instance has to be modified for every wizard page added to a wizard, since each new wizard page acts as *Concrete Factory*.

This task is performed using the *pattern instance wizard*. The menu sequence to start the wizard is *Tools→UML-F Tools→Pattern Instance Wizard*. The wizard is very similar to the *pattern annotation wizard* whose function has bee explained in section 7.2. The only differences are that on the first page the user has to select a pattern instance instead of a pattern (see figure 7.6 on page 141 for a similar wizard page), and that the fields on the *instance name selection page* and on the *model element selection page* are already filled with the chosen pattern instance's properties. Any changes in these properties are performed when the wizard is closed using the *Finish* button.

7.5 Summary

The figures 7.11 to 7.15 on pages 143–145 show the annotated class diagrams for all three pattern instances of the wizard framelet. Namely these are Page Activation Notification, which is a Hook-Object instance, Button Action Notification, which is also a Hook-Object instance, and Page Content Creation, which is an instance of the Abstract Factory pattern. Both visualization notations provided by the PANEX tool, the *pattern mapping notation* and the *pattern marker notation*, are used to highlight the roles certain model elements play in these pattern instances.

As can be seen in the diagrams, the pattern roles are clearly highlighted in both notations. The diagrammatic representation of pattern instances is very intuitive. Thus, while the readability of the diagrams is not affected, the information content of the annotated diagram is by far higher compared to the plain class diagrams, as can be seen in figure 6.11 on page 130, for example.

The user interface provided by the PANEX tool has a clear structure and is easy to use. Wizards guide the user through the more complex tasks of managing pattern instances and creating visualizations. This is of great value to unexperienced users. In addition, also advanced developers can use them efficiently, since the pragmatic approach the wizards follow does not affect the effort needed to perform one of these tasks.

In summary, the diagrams produced by using the PANEX tool are valuable for the documentation of the wizard framelet. Due to the fact that the tool is easy to use, the effort needed to produce the diagrams was rather small, compared to the time it took to produce the overall framelet documentation.

CHAPTER 8

Case Study: TDL Compiler

The second case study, demonstrating the value provided by PANEX, is the documentation of the plug-in interface of a compiler for time behavior specifications in the real-time control applications domain.

In this chapter, first a very brief introduction to the compiler's application domain is given. Second, the plug-in interface is documented using annotated class diagrams produced by PANEX. Third, the advantages and limits of the resulting documentation are discussed.

8.1   TDL Compiler Introduction

The Timing Definition Language (TDL) is a high-level textual notation that is used to specify the timing behavior of hard real-time control applications. Its fundamental idea is to separate the timing aspect of such applications from their functionality. This separation allows the writing of platform independent timing models that may be implemented on an open set of target platforms. TDL, a so-called *software description language*, is specified in the *TDL Specification and Report* document [Tem04a].

TDL programs are purely declarative. All imperative parts of a control application must be provided separately using an imperative programming language such as Java, C or C++.

The *TDL Compiler* is part of the *TDL tool chain*. It takes TDL programs as input and generates executable *Embedded Machine Code (E-Code)*. In addition, platform specific code might be generated. For that purpose, the compiler provides an interface for plug-ins that generate the code specific to the application's target platform. This can be, for instance, *glue code* for invoking the control application's functionality code, or a schedule specification for a certain data bus. See Templ's lecture notes for a detailed discussion of the TDL tool chain [Tem04c, pp. 17–19].

The *TDL Development Kit* (*TDK*), which is available online [TDK04], includes the TDL Compiler, its API documentation in JavaDoc format and a tutorial [Tem04b].

8.2   TDL Compiler Plug-In Interface

Figure 8.1 shows the package diagram of the emcore package, which is the core TDK package. The packages tdlc and platform contain the compiler and the provided platform specific plug-ins. These two packages are discussed in this section. For further information on the other packages, refer to the TDK API documentation [TDK04].

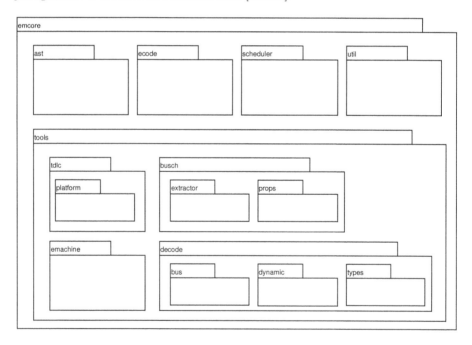

Figure 8.1: emcore package diagram

emcore.tools.tdlc

The package emcore.tools.tdlc contains the classes for the TDL compiler. They are depicted in
the class diagram in figure 8.2.

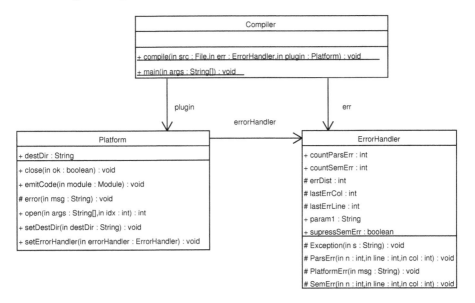

Figure 8.2: emcore.tools.tdlc class diagram

Compiler is the compiler's main class. It provides two public and static methods. The main
method is the entry point for the command line interface of the TDL compiler. The syntax
for the command line options is described in the *TDL Tutorial* [Tem04b]. This method parses
command line parameters and loads the specified platform specific plug-in. Then the plug-in
is initialized, the TDL code is compiled, and the plug-in is invoked in order to generate the
platform specific code. The second method, compile, is intended as interface for tools that want
to invoke the TDL compiler programmatically. It is also used by the main method for invoking
the given plug-in.

The interface specification for platform specific plug-ins is provided by the class platform. This
is a concrete class rather than an interface or an abstract class because it provides the default
implementation for an *empty* plug-in, i.e. a plug-in that does not generate anything. The
methods provided by platform can be categorized by three categories. The *life-cycle methods*
open and close are used for initialization and destruction, respectively. *Generation methods*

are called for every single Module[1] that is processed by the compiler. These are setDestDir, setErrorHandler and emitCode. The *convenience method* error is a shortcut method for reporting generation errors to the compiler using the provided errorHandler.

ErrorHandler provides the functionality of reporting errors to the TDL compiler. Different types of errors are distinguished. Parser exceptions are reported through the Exception method, syntax errors that are found during parsing of a source file are reported via ParsErr, all semantic errors detected are reported using the SemErr method, and the platform specific plug-ins have to use PlatformErr to report any problem to the compiler.

emcore.tools.tdlc.platform

The emcore.tools.tdlc.platform package contains a set of TDL compiler plug-ins for the standard platforms supported by the TDK. They are shown in the class diagram in figure 8.3. It is worth mentioning that the behavior of the BusPlatform plug-in itself can be adapted with plug-ins. In the class diagram, this is depicted by the nodePlatform association. Section 8.2.4 discusses this feature in detail.

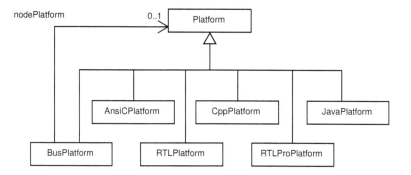

Figure 8.3: emcore.tools.tdlc.platform class diagram

---

[1]The Module class resides in the package emcore.ast and is the root of the compiler's abstract syntax tree representation. This package, however, is not covered in the case study discussion and thus the reader is referred to the TDK API documentation for further information [TDK04].

8.2.1 Plug-In Initialization and Command Line Processing

The life-cycle methods of platform specific plug-ins are used to initialize them (open) and to notify them when the compiler run has finished (close). These methods are called by the compiler's main method if its command line interface is used. When the compiler's API function compile is used to start the compiler, the calling program is responsible for the correct initialization and destruction of the plug-ins.

One of the design goals for the TDL compiler was to achieve extremely high flexibility in the platforms supported. Thus, the plug-in interface is an integral part of the design. To allow for an even more flexible use of the plug-ins, they are allowed to be parameterized using command line parameters. In other words, plug-ins can consume command line parameters. This design decision manifests in the parameters of the init method as well as in its return value. The first parameter, args, contains all parameters given in the command line. idx is the index of the first command line parameter that might be consumed by the plug-in. The init method's semantic defines that its return value specifies the index of the command line parameter succeeding the last parameter consumed by the plug-in. An implication of this semantic is that the method's return value has to be equal to the value of idx in case the plug-in does not consume any command line parameters.

Using this command line processing mechanism allows any plug-in to consume as many command line parameters as needed.

8.2.2 Platform Code Generation

In the design of the platform specific code generation, the *Strategy* pattern is employed. This pattern's purpose is to *"define a family of algorithms, encapsulate each one, and make them interchangeable"* [GHJV95]. Thus, the algorithm can be varied independently of the clients that use it.

For the purpose of the TDL compiler, the *algorithm* is the generation of platform specific code. Figure 8.4 on the next page shows an annotated class diagram in *pattern mapping notation* that depicts the strategy pattern's structure and its relation to the TDL compiler's plug-in interface. As exemplary ConcreteStrategy the class emcore.tools.tdlc.platform.JavaPlatform is used.

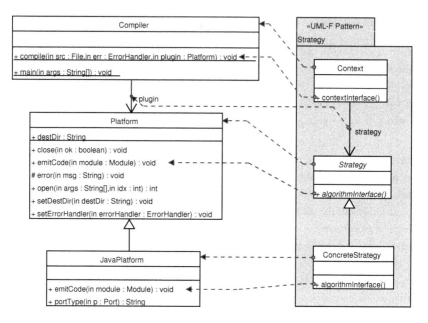

Figure 8.4: Code generation class diagram – Strategy pattern mapping

The Compiler class represents the Context, which means it is the algorithm's client that invokes the concrete algorithm in its compile method. The algorithm's interface, i.e. the *Strategy* class, is represented by the Platform class, and the interface method is called emitCode. Every platform specific plug-in represents a ConcreteStrategy that implements the algorithm interface method emitCode. In other words, the code generation task is performed in this method.

Figure 8.5 on the facing page shows this instance of the Strategy pattern, using the *pattern marker notation*, for all plug-ins provided by the TDK. The UML-F tags used in the diagram are defined in appendix A.4.11 (table A.18 on page 182).

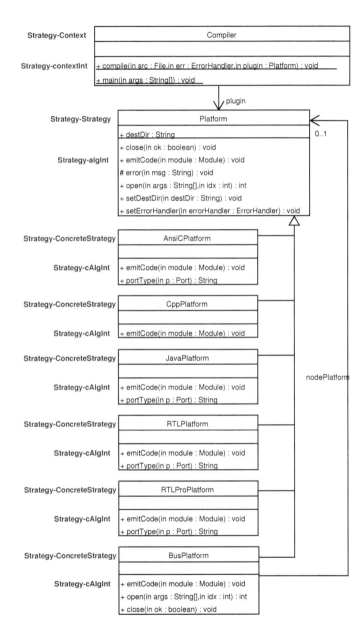

Figure 8.5: Code generation class diagram – Strategy pattern markers

As discussed in section 1.1.2, the Strategy pattern is a specialization of the Hook-Object construction principle (see table 1.2 on page 12). The class diagram in figure 8.6 shows the Strategy pattern instance for code generation, viewed at the *essential construction principles layer*.

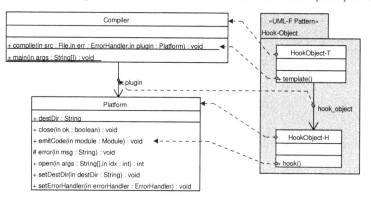

Figure 8.6: Code generation class diagram – Hook-Object mapping

8.2.3   Error Handling

The TDL compiler is designed to be run as a stand-alone program by using the command line interface, or to be integrated in a development environment. Integration of a compiler in such an environment usually requires two interfaces. First, an interface is needed to invoke the compiler. The compile method of the Compiler class provides this functionality. Second, the errors occurring during a compiler run have to be reported to the environment. Ideally, the error messages are enriched with explicit information of the exact position in the source code that causes the problem. The ErrorHandler class provides this interface for the TDL compiler. Errors detected by the scanner and the parser are reported through the ParsErr, SemErr and Exception methods.

For platform specific plug-ins, the base class Platform already provides the error method that can be used to report errors using the ErrorHandler's PlatformErr method. The essential construction principle employed for this variation point is the Hook-Object principle. Figure 8.7 on the facing page shows an annotated class diagram that depicts this relation.

The template role is played by the Platform's error method and the hook role is played by the PlatformErr method of the ErrorHandler class. This class already provides the default behavior that is desired if the compiler's command line interface is used; it prints all error messages to the console, i.e. to the java.lang.System.out stream.

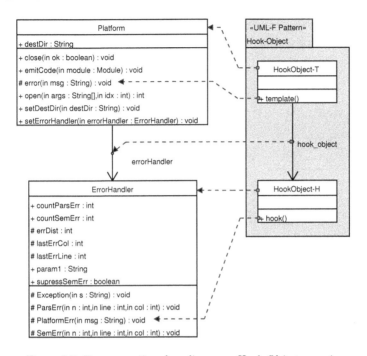

Figure 8.7: Error reporting class diagram – Hook-Object mapping

For an integration of the TDL compiler into a development environment, the ErrorHandler has
to be subclassed and this class has to be passed as parameter to the compile method of the
Compiler class.

8.2.4   Bus-Scheduling Plug-In Interface

A special platform plug-in is the BusPlatform class. The purpose of this plug-in is to generate
schedule specifications for data buses used in distributed real-time control applications. In
the general case, several computation nodes, actuators, and sensors are connected through a
common data bus in a distributed application. In order to ensure the system's time behavior
specification given as input to the TDL compiler, a fulfilling bus schedule has to be found, or,
in case this is not possible for the specified scheduling policy, an error has to be reported. In
addition, the timing code and the platform specific code for the computing nodes have to be
generated.

For that purpose, the **BusPlatform** plug-in itself can load another platform specific plug-in to generate the code for a certain computing node of the distributed system. An overview of the resulting TDL tool chain is given in the lecture notes by Coste and Templ [CT04, p. 34]. The recursive structure forms an instance of the *Composite* pattern [GHJV95]. Figure 8.8 depicts this by using the pattern mapping notation.

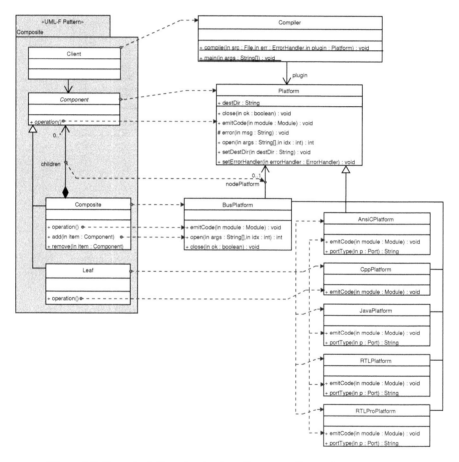

Figure 8.8: Bus scheduling plug-in class diagram – Composite pattern mapping

The **Compiler** class can be identified as **Client** of the composite structure. **Platform** declares the interface for elements in the composite structure, i.e. it plays the **Component** role, and its emitCode operation is used by the client to perform the code generation task in a recursive manner.

The bus scheduling plug-in plays the Composite role of the pattern. It is interesting to note that the pattern's add method is implemented in the plug-in's open method; the plug-in loaded by BusPlatform is specified as command line argument. Furthermore, also the loaded plug-in can consume an arbitrary number of command line arguments. This is made possible by the command line processing mechanism used in the TDL compiler, as described in section 8.2.1. Since it is not necessary to remove a plug-in from the bus scheduling plug-in, the remove role of the pattern is not played by any method of BusPlatform. The pattern's leaf role is played by all other plug-in classes.

A second pattern instance can be identified in the TDL compiler's bus scheduling plug-in. In a similar way the *Strategy* pattern was used in section 8.2.2 to separate the generation of platform specific code from the generation of E-Code, the BusPlatform plug-in uses this pattern to separate the generation of platform specific code for computing nodes from the generation of bus schedules. The class diagram in figure 8.9 on the following page shows this pattern instance using PANEX's pattern marker notation.

In this Strategy pattern instance, the bus scheduling plug-in BusPlatform plays the Context role. In other words, it is the generation strategy's client class. The strategy interface is defined by the Platform class, and all other plug-ins play the ConcreteStrategy role.

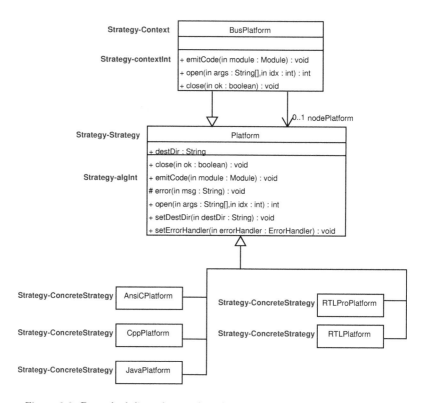

Figure 8.9: Bus scheduling plug-in class diagram – Strategy pattern markers

8.3   Discussion

The case study presented in this chapter shows that the annotated class diagrams produced by PANEX are helpful in understanding framework architectures.

Explicit documentation of the pattern instances that build the foundation of the TDL compiler's plug-in interface complements the plain developer documentation which is part of the TDK in a beneficial way [TDK04]. They document the designer's basic intents and are especially useful to plug-in developers already familiar with design patterns. In particular, the annotation of the *Strategy* pattern in section 8.2.2 and the *Composite* pattern in section 8.2.4 provide useful information. In the original API documentation, which is available in JavaDoc format, none of these concepts is mentioned explicitly. Thus, it takes some extra time for a developer to discover these concepts. With the annotated class diagrams at hand, the code generation interaction pattern as well as the composition structure used by the bus scheduling plug-in becomes clear to everyone with basic knowledge of these design patterns. Anyone else can find explanations of these patterns in several books and on the internet quite easily.

In addition, this case study shows the importance of the availability of essential construction principles in a pattern library. The flexibility in reporting error messages, as documented in section 8.2.3, is not directly supported by any of the catalog patterns [GHJV95]. Simply put, these patterns are too specialized as that they can be used in this context. The more abstract notion of the *Hook-Object* construction principle, however, allows to explicitly highlight this important framework hot spot.

Another aspect that can be seen in this case study is the difference in the two notations provided by PANEX. The *pattern mapping notation* highlights the pattern roles in a very clear and intuitive way. Furthermore, the inclusion of the pattern's structure in the diagrams eases the understanding of the pattern's basic intend, since usually not all developers are familiar with design patterns equally well. Due to the rather large amount of space consumed by the pattern structure itself; this notation is best suited for small and mid-sized class diagrams. On the other hand, the *pattern marker notation* is advantageous if used for large diagrams, like the one shown in figure 8.5 on page 155. Due to the rather small size of the pattern markers, the emphasis of these diagrams is on the framework's structure. However, intimate knowledge of the underlying pattern is necessary to benefit most from that notation. In the end, both notations complement each other and usage of both notations should bring the best results.

CHAPTER 9

Related Work And Conclusion

9.1 Related Work

The purpose of this section is to give a brief overview of alternative approaches of annotating UML diagrams to highlight the patterns used as basis for the design, and alternative approaches for documenting framework architectures.

9.1.1 Design Pattern Annotation in UML

A UML profile for visualizing design patterns is presented by Dong and Yang [DY03]. The profile consists of the fixed set of stereotypes «*PatternClass*», «*PatternAttribute*», «*PatternOperation*», and «*PatternStateMachine*», and each stereotype has a tagged value named pattern. The tagged values are strings of a fixed format that allows for the uniform specification of pattern name, instance identifier, and pattern role for the stereotyped mode element. In addition, several constraints are defined in the profile. The profile uses the extension mechanism of UML 1.4 and thus is not compliant to the UML 2.0 standard.

Adams and Sanada present an approach that uses two separate UML profiles, one profile for design patterns, and another profile for frameworks [SA02]. Both are used together to annotate the patterns that were used for the framework design. The pattern profile defines the four stereotypes «*InstanceClass*», «*ForAllNewMethods*», «*Hook*», and «*Template*», and the tags

extensible, instantiation, and final. In addition, an adaptation of the *UML collaboration* notation can be used to highlight pattern roles.

The framework profile also defines a fixed set of stereotypes («*ApplicationClass*», «*ForAll-
NewMethods*», «*Hook*», and «*Template*») and tagged values (variation, extensible, binding,
instantiation, final, and PatternName-role).

The authors also distinguish class diagrams according to their granularity. In other words, class
diagrams are categorized either as *design class diagram (DCD)*, as *detailed DCD* or as *design
pattern class diagram*. The proposed UML extensions are not compliant to version 2 of the
UML. As proof of concept, the proposed UML extensions have been implemented in a CASE
tool.

Dong investigates several extensions to UML that are used for explicit representation of individual design patterns in a composition of patterns and shows their shortcomings [Don02]. In
the *Venn diagram-style*, the diagram background is shaded in such a way that classes part of a
certain pattern are located on top of the particular shade, which is a closed area.

The *dotted bounding* notation is similar to the Venn diagram style notation, but the shades are
replaced by dashed lines that mark the boundary of a pattern's area.

The third notation examined is the *UML collaboration* notation. The standard UML notation
[OMG03d, chapter 9] is used in *composite structure diagrams*. Dashed ellipses with pattern
names inside are used to represent patterns, i.e. these are the collaborations. Dashed lines are
used to associate the patterns to the participating classes, which is called *roleBinding* in UML.
The idea of the so-called *pattern:role* notation is to tag classes with a shaded box containing
the pattern and/or role name associated with the class, separated by a semicolon.

The author also proposes a new notation, the *tagged pattern* notation, which is designed to
overcome the shortcomings of the other notations presented, which is that there are no possibilities of annotating pattern roles for operations and attributes. The notation uses tagged
values that are used to hold pattern and/or participant names for the corresponding classes
and its operations and attributes. In addition, an alternative representation for the tagged
pattern notation is proposed that uses a separate compartment for each class and that is used
to hold pattern-related information. This way, the author argues, pattern related information
is treated as first-class members in the same way as attributes and operations of a class are.

The work presented by Yacoub and Ammar is based on designing a system as a composition of
design patterns [YA01]. Stereotypes for packages are used to depict the patterns used for the
design.

Another solution for annotating design diagrams with pattern roles by using tags is described
by Riehle and Gross [RG98]. The authors propose the use of role diagrams for documenting
class interactions. However, these diagrams are not part of UML and thus this extension is not

compliant to the standard. Moreover, role diagrams do not model variation points explicitly, which is essential for the documentation of framework architectures.

9.1.2   Framework Hot Spot Documentation

In standard UML notation, frameworks are represented as packages stereotyped «*framework*» that assemble classes, patterns, and templates. They represent reusable architectures for all or parts of a system [OMG03d, appendix B]. Collaboration diagrams can be used for documenting framework adaptation, but this notation lacks in possibilities of describing interdependencies among variation points.

A design method for frameworks is presented by Bouassida et al. [BBAGBH04]. It includes a UML profile called *F-UML*. Tagged values and graphical annotations are used to distinguish between the framework core classes and hot spot classes. The visual representation of a variation point emphasizes the distinction between white-box and black-box hot spots. For example, a highlighted class border indicates a core framework class, while a filled square in the top-right corner of a class indicates a variation point. The square's fill color distinguishes the hot spot type; grey indicates a white-box hot spot, and black indicates a black-box hot spot. In addition, the authors define well-formedness rules that are used to guide the construction of a correct design.

F-UML defines extensions for use case diagrams, class diagrams, and sequence diagrams. A prototypical implementation of the F-UML approach also is presented.

The Catalysis approach [DW98] uses the UML notation and proposes a design method based on frameworks and components. It focuses on modeling and specifying reusable components using UML and the Object Constraint Language. *Type models* are the basis for defining a type. *Collaborations* are partial definitions of how typed objects interact when playing a certain role. Individual types and collaborations can be refined using *refinements*. *Frameworks* are defined as generic units of modeling or design, and a *framework collaboration* is a particular kind of framework that utilizes placeholder types and generalized actions to permit flexible composition.

9.2   Concluding Remarks

In thus book, the theoretical foundations of frameworks and patterns were discussed in chapter 1, and chapter 2 presented a new version of the *UML Profile for Framework Architectures* that is compatible to UML version 2.0. This UML-F profile uses the same concepts as the original profile [FPR01]. The usage of the revised UML profile mechanism, however, made it necessary to change the profile's structure and to redefine the tag definition mechanism. Furthermore, some ambiguities of the original profile have been removed and the *Composite* , *Decorator*, and *Chain-of-Responsibility* patterns are now present in the construction principles layer as well as in the pattern layer. This better highlights their double roles as patterns and construction principles, and also leaves the choice on which level of abstraction they are used in an annotated framework to the profile's user.

The main part of this book describes the development of the *PANEX* tool. The whole development process, starting with the analysis of the user needs in chapter 3, including the requirements analysis in chapter 4 and the evaluation of the underlying CASE tool in chapter 5, up to the description of the tool's software design with some implementation details in chapter 6, is documented.

PANEX is implemented in Java as plug-in to ArgoUML, which is an open-source UML CASE tool. The complete UML-F metamodel is supported by the tool. Due to the fact that ArgoUML only supports the UML version 1.3, a new mechanism has been introduced for the definition of the profile's pattern library. This mechanism easily can be used to define domain specific patterns – a critical aspect for the usefulness of a UML-F based tool.

The tool provides support for the framework developer to annotate the framework's software architecture with UML-F tags. A comfortable, wizard-based user interface guides through the annotation process. Two different visualization notations for the annotation of class diagrams have been implemented. A wizard helps the framework developer as well as the framework user to enrich existing class diagrams with visualizations of the patterns and construction principles used. Moreover, the visualizations generated can be of different levels of abstraction, such as the essential construction principles layer or the pattern layer, and also the details shown can be customized.

PANEX's usability is demonstrated in the case study in chapter 7. A tutorial-like style is used to show the tool's features and their usage. The case study, which is a user interface wizard framelet developed for PANEX itself, shows the tool's applicability to frameworks in the user interface domain.

In the second case study, the plug-in interface of a compiler for time behavior specifications in the real-time control applications domain is documented using PANEX. This case study, which was presented in chapter 8, shows the usability of the pattern annotated diagrams. They are used to document the interaction patterns and the structural composition used to generate platform specific code. In addition, the importance of the essential construction principles to document framework hot spots that are not covered by any design pattern is shown.

Summarizing up, it can be seen that the UML-F profile and the annotation of essential construction principles and design patterns is a useful approach for documenting framework architectures. The importance of tool support for such an approach has been shown, and the PANEX tool fulfills the stated requirements. It allows for the convenient annotation of design patterns and the generation of adequate design diagrams using two different notations. Every notation has its own advantages and disadvantages. Together, they provide support for documenting the designer's basic intentions in a way that is beneficial for both, the developer of a framework and also its user.

Part IV

Appendix

***

PANEX UML-F Library Reference

***

This appendix provides a quick reference to the UML-F library that is part of the PANEX distribution. The library is located in the file `PANEX UML-F Library Template.zargo` and can be used as basis for design pattern annotation projects using the PANEX tool extension for ArgoUML.

All library packages, pattern packages, and tag definitions provided in the UML-F library are listed in the subsequent sections. The chapter is structured analogous to the library's package hierarchy.

Tag Definition Format

A tabular form is used for listing the UML-F tag definitions. The meaning of the columns is defined as follows:

Tag name: Specifies the tag name. Aliases for the tag are also listed, separated by commas.

In the UML-F library model, the tag name and aliases are specified using the tagged value UML-F `TagDef`.

Applies to: Lists the model element types the tag can be applied to.

In the UML-F library model, this property is specified using the tagged value UML-F `TagApplication`.

Expansion: Lists the tags this tag can be expanded to.

In the UML-F library model, the expansion relationship between tags is specified using the tagged value UML-F TagExpansion.

Defining Element: Specifies the model element in the UML-F library model that contains the tag definition.

A.1   UML-F Basic Library

This is the root package of the UML-F library. In its namespace, the following library packages are defined:

Basic Modeling Layer	(see section A.2)
Essential Construction Principles Layer	(see section A.3 on the next page)
Pattern Layer	(see section A.4 on page 176)

A.2   Basic Modeling Layer

The UML-F Tags defined in this library package are listed in table A.1.

Table A.1: Basic Modeling Layer tags

Tag name	Applies to	Expansion	Defining Element
application	*all*	—	application
framework	*all*	—	framework
utility	*all*	—	utility
fixed	*all*	—	fixed
adapt-static	*all*	—	adapt-static
adapt-dyn	*all*	—	adapt-dyn

A.2.1   Template-Hook Tags

The UML-F Tags defined in this pattern package are listed in table A.2.

Table A.2: Template-Hook tags

Tag name	Applies to	Expansion	Defining Element
Hook, H	Interface, Class	—	Hook
hook, h	Operation	—	Hook::hook
Template, T	Interface, Class	—	Template
template, t	Operation	—	Template::template

A.3   Essential Construction Principles Layer

A.3.1   Hook-Method

The UML-F Tags defined in this pattern package are listed in table A.3.

Table A.3: Hook-Method tags

Tag name	Applies to	Expansion	Defining Element
HookMethod-TH, HM-TH	Class	Template, Hook	HookMethod-TH
HookMethod-t, HM-t	Operation	template	HookMethod-TH::template
HookMethod-h, HM-h	Operation	hook	HookMethod-TH::hook

A.3.2   Hook-Object

The UML-F Tags defined in this pattern package are listed in table A.4.

Table A.4: Hook-Object tags

Tag name	Applies to	Expansion	Defining Element
HookObject-T, HO-T	Interface, Class	Template	HookObject-T
HookObject-t, HO-t	Operation	template	HookObject-T::template
HookObject-H, HO-H	Interface, Class	Hook	HookObject-H
HookObject-h, HO-h	Operation	hook	HookObject-H::hook
HookObject-Ref, HO-R	Association	—	hook_object

A.3.3   Chain-Of-Responsibility

The UML-F Tags defined in this pattern package are listed in table A.5.

Table A.5: Chain-Of-Responsibility tags

Tag name	Applies to	Expansion	Defining Element
COR-TH	Class	Template, Hook	ChainOfResponsibility_TH
COR-th	Operation	template, hook	ChainOfResponsibility_TH:: template_hook
COR-successor	Association	—	successor

A.3.4 Composite

The UML-F Tags defined in this pattern package are listed in table A.6.

Table A.6: Composite tags

Tag name	Applies to	Expansion	Defining Element
Composite-H	Interface, Class	Hook	Composite_H
Composite-h	Operation	hook	Composite_H::template_hook
Composite-T	Class	Template	Composite_T
Composite-t	Operation	template	Composite_T::template_hook
Composite-Leaf	Class	Hook	Composite_Leaf
Composite-children	Association	—	children

A.3.5 Decorator

The UML-F Tags defined in this pattern package are listed in table A.7.

Table A.7: Decorator tags

Tag name	Applies to	Expansion	Defining Element
Decorator-H	Interface, Class	Hook	Decorator_H
Decorator-h	Operation	hook	Decorator_H::template_hook
Decorator-T	Class	Template	Decorator_T
Decorator-t	Operation	template	Decorator_T::template_hook
Decorator-comp	Association	—	component

A.4 Pattern Layer

A.4.1 Factory Method

The UML-F Tags defined in this pattern package are listed in table A.8.

Table A.8: Factory Method tags

Tag name	Applies to	Expansion	Defining Element
FacM-Product	Interface, Class	—	Product
FacM-ConcreteProduct	Class	—	ConcreteProduct
FacM-Creator	Class	HookMethod-TH	Creator
FacM-facM	Operation	HookMethod-h	Creator::factoryMethod
FacM-anOp	Operation	HookMethod-t	Creator::anOperation
FacM-ConcreteCreator	Class	—	ConcreteCreator
FacM-cFacM	Operation	—	ConcreteCreator:: factoryMethod

A.4.2 Template Method

The UML-F Tags defined in this pattern package are listed in table A.9.

Table A.9: Template Method tags

Tag name	Applies to	Expansion	Defining Element
TemplateM-AbstractClass	Class	HookMethod-TH	AbstractClass
TemplateM-templateM	Operation	HookMethod-t	AbstractClass:: templateMethod
TemplateM-primitiveOp	Operation	HookMethod-h	AbstractClass:: primitiveOperation
TemplateM-ConcreteClass	Class	—	ConcreteClass
TemplateM-cPrimitiveOp	Operation	—	ConcreteClass:: primitiveOperation

A.4.3   Abstract Factory

The UML-F Tags defined in this pattern package are listed in table A.10.

Table A.10: Abstract Factory tags

Tag name	Applies to	Expansion	Defining Element
AbstractFactory-Client, AF-Client	Interface, Class	HookObject-T	Client
AbstractFactory-clientM, AF-clientM	Operation	HookObject-t	Client::clientMethod
AbstractFactory-AbstractProduct, AF-AbstractProduct	Interface, Class	—	AbstractProduct
AbstractFactory-ConcreteProduct, AF-ConcreteProduct	Class	—	ConcreteProduct
AbstractFactory-AbstractFactory, AF-AbstractFactory	Interface, Class	HookObject-H	AbstractFactory
AbstractFactory-createProduct, AF-createProduct	Operation	HookObject-h	AbstractFactory:: createProduct
AbstractFactory-ConcreteFactory, AF-ConcreteFactory	Class	—	ConcreteFactory
AbstractFactory-cCreateProduct, AF-cCreateProduct	Operation	—	ConcreteFactory:: createProduct
AbstractFactory-factory, AF-fac	Association	HookObject-Ref	factory
AbstractFactory-product, AF-prod	Association	—	product

A.4.4 Bridge

The UML-F Tags defined in this pattern package are listed in table A.11.

Table A.11: Bridge tags

Tag name	Applies to	Expansion	Defining Element
Bridge-Abstraction	Interface, Class	HookObject-T	Abstraction
Bridge-operation	Operation	HookObject-t	Abstraction::operation
Bridge-Implementor	Interface, Class	HookObject-H	Implementor
Bridge-operationImp	Operation	HookObject-h	Implementor::operationImp
Bridge-ConcreteImplementor	Class	—	ConcreteImplementor
Bridge-cOperationImp	Operation	—	ConcreteImplementor:: operationImp
Bridge-imp	Association	HookObject-Ref	imp

A.4.5 Builder

The UML-F Tags defined in this pattern package are listed in table A.12.

Table A.12: Builder tags

Tag name	Applies to	Expansion	Defining Element
Builder-Director	Interface, Class	HookObject-T	Director
Builder-construct	Operation	HookObject-t	Director::construct
Builder-Builder	Interface, Class	HookObject-H	Builder
Builder-buildPart	Operation	HookObject-h	Builder::buildPart
Builder-ConcreteBuilder	Class	—	ConcreteBuilder
Builder-cBuildPart	Operation	—	ConcreteBuilder::buildPart
Builder-builder	Association	HookObject-Ref	builder

A.4.6   Command

The UML-F Tags defined in this pattern package are listed in table A.13.

Table A.13: Command tags

Tag name	Applies to	Expansion	Defining Element
Command-Invoker	Interface, Class	HookObject-T	Invoker
Command-clientM	Operation	HookObject-t	Invoker::clientMethod
Command-Command	Interface, Class	HookObject-H	Command
Command-execute	Operation	HookObject-h	Command::execute
Command-ConcreteCommand	Class	—	ConcreteCommand
Command-cExecute	Operation	—	ConcreteCommand::execute
Command-cmd	Association	HookObject-Ref	command

A.4.7 Interpreter

The UML-F Tags defined in this pattern package are listed in table A.14.

Table A.14: Interpreter tags

Tag name	Applies to	Expansion	Defining Element
Interpreter-Client	Interface, Class	HookObject-T	Client
Interpreter-clientM	Operation	HookObject-t	Client::clientMethod
Iterpreter-AbstractExpression	Interface, Class	HookObject-H	AbstractExpression
Interpreter-interpret	Operation	HookObject-h	AbstractExpression::interpret
Interpreter-exp	Association	HookObject-Ref	expression
Interpreter-TerminalExpression	Class	—	TerminalExpression
Interpreter-teInterpret	Operation	—	TerminalExpression::interpret
Interpreter-NonterminalExpression	Class	—	NonterminalExpression
Interpreter-nteInterpret	Operation	—	NonterminalExpression:: interpret

A.4.8   Observer

The UML-F Tags defined in this pattern package are listed in table A.15.

Table A.15: Observer tags

Tag name	Applies to	Expansion	Defining Element
Observer-Subject	Interface, Class	HookObject-T	Subject
Observer-notify	Operation	HookObject-t	Subject::notify
Observer-Observer	Interface, Class	HookObject-H	Observer
Observer-update	Operation	HookObject-h	Observer::update
Observer-observers	Association	HookObject-Ref	observers
Observer-ConcreteObserver	Class	—	ConcreteObserver
Observer-cUpdate	Operation	—	ConcreteObserver::update

A.4.9   Prototype

The UML-F Tags defined in this pattern package are listed in table A.16.

Table A.16: Prototype tags

Tag name	Applies to	Expansion	Defining Element
Prototype-Client	Interface, Class	HookObject-T	Client
Prototype-clientM	Operation	HookObject-t	Client::clientMethod
Prototype-Prototype	Interface, Class	HookObject-H	Prototype
Prototype-clone	Operation	HookObject-h	Prototype::clone
Prototype-ConcretePrototype	Class	—	ConcretePrototype
Prototype-cClone	Operation	—	ConcretePrototype::clone
Prototype-proto	Association	HookObject-Ref	prototype

A.4.10   State

The UML-F Tags defined in this pattern package are listed in table A.17.

Table A.17: State tags

Tag name	Applies to	Expansion	Defining Element
State-Context	Interface, Class	HookObject-T	Context
State-request	Operation	HookObject-t	Context::request
State-State	Interface, Class	HookObject-H	State
State-handle	Operation	HookObject-h	State::handle
State-stateref	Association	HookObject-Ref	state
State-ConcreteState	Class	—	ConcreteState
State-cHandle	Operation	—	ConcreteState::handle

A.4.11   Strategy

The UML-F Tags defined in this pattern package are listed in table A.18.

Table A.18: Strategy tags

Tag name	Applies to	Expansion	Defining Element
Strategy-Context	Interface, Class	HookObject-T	Context
Strategy-contextInt	Operation	HookObject-t	Context::contextInterface
Strategy-Strategy	Interface, Class	HookObject-H	Strategy
Strategy-algInt	Operation	HookObject-h	Strategy::algorithmInterface
Strategy-strategyref	Association	HookObject-Ref	strategy
Strategy-ConcreteStrategy	Class	—	ConcreteStrategy
Strategy-cAlgInt	Operation	—	ConcreteStrategy:: algorithmInterface

A.4.12   Chain-Of-Responsibility

The UML-F Tags defined in this pattern package are listed in table A.19.

Table A.19: Chain-Of-Responsibility tags

Tag name	Applies to	Expansion	Defining Element
COR-Client	Interface, Class	—	Client
COR-Handler	Class	COR-TH	Handler
COR-handleRequest	Operation	COR-th	Handler::handleRequest
COR-ConcreteHandler	Class	COR-TH	ConcreteHandler
COR-cHandleRequest	Operation	COR-th	ConcreteHandler:: handleRequest
COR-successor	Association	COR-successor	successor

A.4.13   Composite

The UML-F Tags defined in this pattern package are listed in table A.20.

Table A.20: Composite tags

Tag name	Applies to	Expansion	Defining Element
Composite-Client	Interface, Class	—	Client
Composite-Component	Interface, Class	Composite-H	Component
Composite-op	Operation	Composite-h	Component::operation
Composite-Composite	Class	Composite-T	Composite
Composite-cOp	Operation	Composite-t	Composite::operation
Composite-add	Operation	—	Composite::add
Composite-remove	Operation	—	Composite::remove
Composite-Leaf	Class	Composite-Leaf	Leaf
Composite-lOp	Operation	—	Leaf::operation
Composite-children	Association	Composite-children	children

A.4.14 Decorator

The UML-F Tags defined in this pattern package are listed in table A.21.

Table A.21: Decorator tags

Tag name	Applies to	Expansion	Defining Element
Decorator-Component	Interface, Class	Decorator-H	Component
Decorator-operation	Operation	Decorator-h	Component::operation
Decorator-Decorator	Class	Decorator-T	Decorator
Decorator-dOperation	Operation	Decorator-t	Decorator::operation
Decorator-ConcreteComponent	Class	—	ConcreteComponent
Decorator-cOperation	Operation	—	ConcreteComponent::operation
Decorator-component	Association	Decorator-comp	component

C

Component Object Model (COM)

A specification by Microsoft Corporation that describes a software architecture for building component-based applications.

(*See page 99*)

Computer Aided Software Engineering (CASE)

A research field dealing with tool support for software engineering and programming related tasks.

(*See page 31*)

E

Embedded Machine Code (E-Code)

Binary code that can be executed by a virtual machine. This so-called *Embedded Machine (E-Machine)* ensures the correct runtime behavior of a realtime control application specified by a TDL program.

(*See page 149*)

Extensible Markup Language (XML)

A markup language for structuring arbitrary data. XML is a simple dialect of SGML designed for ease of implementation and for interoperability with both SGML and HTML. It is an open, vendor-neutral, and OS-independent recommendation by the

W3C.

(See page 190)

F

Framework (FW)

"Semi-finished pieces of software" that are extensible through the *callback-style* of programming [FPR02, p. 188].

"A (generative) architecture designed for maximum reuse, represented as a collective set of abstract and concrete classes; encapsulated potential behavior for subclassed specializations."[Mat96, p. 52].

(See page 19)

G

Gang of Four (GoF)

Jargon expression to tag the authors of the first book on design patterns: Erich Gamma, Richard Helm, Ralph Johnson and John Vlissides [GHJV95].

(See page 4)

H

HyperText Markup Language (HTML)

A simple markup language used to create hypertext documents that are portable from one platform to another. HTML documents are SGML documents with generic semantics. The language is specified in a W3C recommendation.

(See page 185)

I

Institute of Electrical and Electronic Engineers (IEEE)

Organization that promotes the engineering process of creating, developing, integrating, sharing, and applying knowledge about electro and information technologies and sciences. Founded in 1963.

International Electrotechnical Commission (IEC)

The IEC is the standards organization for all areas of electrotechnology. It was officially founded in June 1906.

(*See page 91*)

International Organization for Standardization (ISO)

Organization that develops international standards for production and quality. The ISO started its operation in February 1947.

(*See page 91*)

J

Java Virtual Machine (JVM)

A virtual machine for the Java platform that makes compiled java code independent from any hardware architecture.

(*See page 100*)

M

Meta Object Facility (MOF)

A OMG standard that defines a conceptual framework for describing meta-data [OMG03a].

(*See page 33*)

Metaclass

A class whose instances are classes [OMG03e].

(*See page 35*)

N

North Atlantic Treaty Organization (NATO)

International organization for cooperative defense against aggression. Established in 1949.

(*See page 3*)

O

Object-Based

In contrast to the OT paradigm, the object-based paradigm is based on information hiding and encapsulation only.

Object Constraint Language (OCL)

A formal language used to describe expressions on UML models. These expressions typically specify invariant conditions that must hold for the system being modeled or queries over objects described in a model. OCL is a OMG standard [OMG03b]. *(See page 34)*

Object Engineering Process (OEP)

A process model for component oriented and object oriented software development [Oes01].
(See page 75)

Object Management Group (OMG)

An international consortium that promotes the theory and practice of object-oriented technology in software development. The OMG, founded in 1989, also acts as standardization board.
(See page 30)

Object-Oriented (OO)

Built upon the *Object Technology (OT)* paradigm.
(See page 5)

Object Technology (OT)

Object technology is a paradigm as well as a research field, and nowadays it is one of the most mature software development technologies [Bur99]. Three essential concepts comprise object technology: information hiding, inheritance with polymorphism, and dynamic binding [PP01].
(See page 4)

P

Pattern Annotation Extension (PANEX)

A CASE-tool extension that allows for the explicit annotation of design patterns in UML class diagrams. The *PANEX* project is described in this book.
(See page 63)

R

Rational Unified Process (RUP)

An iterative and incremental software development process [Kru00, Lar01].

(See page 75)

S

Standard Generalized Markup Language (SGML)

An international standard for describing the data that makes up documents. SGML data is vendor, platform, and media independent. It is standardized by the International Organization for Standardization in standard ISO 8879.

(See page 185)

T

Timing Definition Language (TDL)

A high-level textual notation for defining the timing behavior of real-time control applications [Tem04a].

(See page 149)

U

UML Profile

An extension to the UML that is strictly additive to standard UML semantics.

(See page 29)

UML Profile for Framework Architectures (UML-F)

A UML Profile for object and component frameworks [FPR01]. It supports the description of framework architectures by explicit annotation of design decisions in from of patterns.

(See page 30)

Unified Modeling Language (UML)

UML is a modeling language for object-oriented software systems with a strong emphasis on a graphical representation. It is used for visualizing, specifying, constructing, and documenting the artifacts of an object-oriented software system. The UML is an OMG standard [OMG03c, OMG03d, OMG03e].

(See page 29)

Use Case (UC)

A *"story of using a system"* [Lar01]. A use case is defined as set of actions that, when executed following one after another in sequence, form a certain behavior of the system to be modeled, and whose result is of functional value [JRH+03].

(*See page 75*)

W

World Wide Web Consortium (W3C)

An international consortium that strives to lead the *World Wide Web* to its full potential by developing interoperable technologies, specifications, guidelines, software, and tools. Founded in October 1994.

(*See page 186*)

X

XML Metadata Interchange (XMI)

An open standard based on XML that defines an open information interchange model intended for the interchange of metadata among development tools working with object technology.

(*See page 98*)

List of Figures

List of Tables

Listings Index

Bibliography

[AMC01]   Deepak Alur, Dan Malks, and John Crupi. *Core J2EE Patterns: Best Practices and Design Strategies*. Prentice Hall PTR, Palo Alto, California, 2001.

[App98]   Brad Appleton. Patterns and software: Essential concepts and terminology, August 1998. Available online: `http://www.enteract.com/~bradapp/docs/patterns-intro.html` (cited 2004-12-12).

[Arg05a]   ArgoUML website, 2005. Available online: `http://argouml.tigris.org/` (cited 2005-02-22).

[Arg05b]   Cookbook for Developers of ArgoUML, 2005. Available online: `http://argouml.tigris.org/documentation/defaulthtml/cookbook/` (cited 2005-02-22).

[Azu04]   Motoei Azuma. Applying ISO/IEC 9126-1 quality model to quality requirements engineering on critical software. In *Proceedings of the Third International Workshop on Requirements for High Assurance Systems (RHAS 2004)*, 2004.

[Bau93]   F. L. Bauer. Software engineering – wie es begann. *Informatik Spektrum*, 16(5):259–260, Oktober 1993. In German language.

[BBAGBH04]   N. Bouassida, H. Ben-Abdallah, F. Gargouri, and A. Ben-Hamadou. A UML based framework design method. *Journal of Object Technology*, 3(8):97–119, September-October 2004.

[BBF⁺02]   Pere Botella, Xavier Burgués, Xavier Franch, Mario Huerta, and Guadalupe
             Salazar. Modeling non-functional requirements. In Amador Durán and Miguel
             Toro, editors, *Applying Requirements Engineering*. Catedral Publicaciones, Sala-
             manca, Spain, 2002. (Selected papers from Jornadas de Ingeniería de Requisitos
             Aplicada – JIRA'01).

[BMR⁺96]   Frank Buschmann, Regine Meunier, Hans Rohnert, Peter Sommerlad, and
             Michael Stal. *Pattern-Oriented Software Architecture: A System of Patterns*.
             John Wiley & Sons, Inc., New York, 1996.

[Bur99]   Rainer Burkhardt. *UML - Unified Modeling Language. Objektorienntierte Mod-
             ellierung für die Praxis*. Addison Wesley Longman, 2nd edition, 1999. In German
             language.

[BV01]   Jan Bosch and Jilles Van Gurp. Design, implementation and evolution of object
             oriented frameworks: concepts & guidelines. *Software — Practice and Experi-
             ence*, 31(3):277–300, April 2001.

[Cha05]   Tim Chamillard. Lecture notes for a course on software product assurance,
             Spring 2005. Available online: http://www.cs.uccs.edu/~chamillard/cs536/
             Papers/9126Handout.pdf (cited 2005-02-22).

[CKW⁺99]   Steve Cook, Anneke Kleppe, Jos Warmer, Richard Mitchell, Bernhard Rumpe,
             and Alan Cameron Wills. Defining UML family members using prefaces. In
             Christine Mingins and B. Meyer, editors, *Proceedings of the 32nd International
             Conference on Technology of Object-Oriented Languages (TOOLS 32)*, pages
             102–114. IEEE Computer Society, 1999.

[CLD99]   Peter Coad, Eric Lefebvre, and Jeff De Luca. *Java Modeling in Color with UML*.
             Prentice Hall PTR, New Jersey, 1999.

[CT04]   Emilia Coste and Josef Templ. Distributed, Time-Safe TDL Execution — Con-
             cepts, Tools and Run-time Infrastructure. Lecture notes for a course on dis-
             tributed systems, 2004. Available online: http://www.softwareresearch.net/
             site/teaching/ WS0405/ds/docs/DistributedTDL.pdf (cited 2005-03-18).

[Dij70]   E. W. Dijkstra. Structured programming. In J. N. Buxton and B. Randell,
             editors, *Software Engineering Techniques*, pages 84–87, Brussels, Belgium, 1970.
             Scientific Affairs Division, NATO Science Committee.

[Don02]   Jing Dong. UML extensions for design pattern compositions. *Journal of Object
             Technology*, 1(5):151–163, November-December 2002.

[Dru01]   Peter F. Drucker. *The Essential Drucker.* Harper Business, 2001.

[DW98]   Desmond D'Souza and Alan Cameron Wills. *Objects, Components and Frameworks With UML: The Catalysis Approach.* Addison Wesley, 1998.

[DY03]   Jing Dong and Sheng Yang. Visualizing design patterns with a UML profile. In *IEEE Symposium on Human Centric Computing Languages and Environments (HCC 2003),*, Auckland, New Zealand, October 2003. IEEE Computer Society.

[FFVM04]   Lidia Fuentes-Fernández and Antonio Vallecillo-Moreno. An introduction to UML profiles. *The European Journal for the Informatics Professional (UP-GRADE),* V(2):6–13, April 2004.

[Fir03]   Donald Firesmith. Specifying good requirements. *Journal of Object Technology,* 2(4):77–87, July-August 2003.

[FJ00]   Mohamed E. Fayad and Ralph E. Johnson. *Domain-Specific Application Frameworks: Framework Experience by Industry.* John Wiley & Sons, Inc., New York City, 2000.

[FLA+01]   Marcus Fontoura, Carlos J. Lucena, Alexandre Andreatta, Sérgio E. Carvalho, and Celso C. Ribeiro. Using UML-F to enhance framework development: a case study in the local search heuristics domain. *Journal of Systems and Software,* 57(3):201–206, 2001.

[FPR00]   Marcus Fontoura, Wolfgang Pree, and Bernhard Rumpe. UML-F: A modeling language for object-oriented frameworks. In Elisa Bertino, editor, *Proceedings of the 14th European Conference on Object-Oriented Programing (ECOOP2000),* volume 1850 of *LNCS,* pages 63–83, Sophia Antipolis and Cannes, France, June 2000. Springer-Verlag.

[FPR01]   Marcus Fontoura, Wolfgang Pree, and Bernhard Rumpe. *The UML Profile for Framework Architectures.* Addison Wesley, December 2001.

[FPR02]   Marcus Fontoura, Wolfgang Pree, and Bernhard Rumpe. Product line annotations with UML-F. In *Proceedings of the Second International Conference on Software Product Lines,* pages 188–197, San Diego, California, August 2002.

[FSJ99a]   Mohamed E. Fayad, Douglas C. Schmidt, and Ralph E. Johnson. *Building Application Frameworks: Object-Oriented Foundations of Framework Design.* John Wiley & Sons, Inc., New York City, 1999.

[FSJ99b]   Mohamed E. Fayad, Douglas C. Schmidt, and Ralph E. Johnson. *Implementing Application Frameworks: Object-Oriented Frameworks at Work*. John Wiley & Sons, Inc., New York City 1999.

[Fuj05]   Fujaba website, 2005. Available online: `http://www.fujaba.de/` (cited 2005-02-22).

[GAO95]   David Garlan, Robert Allen, and John Ockerbloom. Architectural mismatch: Why reuse is so hard. *IEEE Software*, 12(6):17–26, November 1995.

[GEF05]   Graphical Editor Framework (GEF) website, 2005. Available online: `http://gef.tigris.org/` (cited 2005-02-22).

[GHJV95]   Erich Gamma, Richard Helm, Ralph Johnson, and John Vlissides. *Design Patterns - Elements of reusable object oriented software*. Addison Wesley, 1st edition, 1995.

[ISO01]   ISO/IEC Standards 9126-1:2001(E), Software Engineering – Product Quality – Part 1: Quality Model, 2001. International Organization for Standardization and International Electrotechnical Commission.

[JRH+03]   Mario Jeckle, Chris Rupp, Jürgen Hahn, Barbara Zengler, and Stefan Queins. *UML 2 glasklar*. Carl Hanser Verlag, November 2003. In German language.

[JUn05]   JUnit website, 2005. Available online: `http://www.junit.org/` (cited 2005-03-01).

[KHB03]   Olaf Kath, Eckhardt Holz, and Marc Born. *Softwareentwicklung mit UML 2*. Addison Wesley, November 2003. In German language.

[Kru95]   Phillippe P. Kruchten. The 4+1 view model of architecture. *IEEE Software*, 12(6):42–50, November 1995.

[Kru00]   Phillippe P. Kruchten. *The Rational Unified Process – An Introduction*. Addison Wesley Longman, second edition, 2000.

[Lar01]   Craig Larman. *Applying UML and Patterns: An Introduction to Object-Oriented Analysis and Design and the Unified Process*. Prentice Hall PTR, second edition, July 2001.

[LCLRC03]   Francisca Losavio, Ledis Chirinos, Nicole Lévy, and Amar Ramdane-Cherif. Quality characteristics for software architecture. *Journal of Object Technology*, 2(2):133–150, March-April 2003.

[Mat96]   Michael Mattsson. *Object-Oriented Frameworks — A survey of methodological issues.* Licentiate thesis, Department of Computer Science, Lund University, Sweden, 1996.

[NR69]   P. Naur and B. Randell, editors. *Software Engineering: Report on a Conference sponsored by the NATO Science Committee, Garmisch, Germany, 7th to 11th October 1968*, Brussels, Belgium, January 1969. Scientific Affairs Division, NATO Science Committee.

[NSU05]   The Novosoft Metadata Framework and UML Library (NSUML) website, 2005. Available online: http://nsuml.sourceforge.net (cited 2005-02-22).

[Oes01]   Bernd Oesterreich. *Objektorientierte Softwareentwicklung: Analyse und Design mit der UML.* R.Oldenbourg, Munich, Germany, July 2001. In German language.

[OMG99]   Object Management Group, Inc. *OMG Unified Modeling Language Specification, Version 1.3*, June 1999.

[OMG03a]   Object Management Group, Inc. *Meta Object Facility (MOF) 2.0 Core Specification*, October 2003. OMG Final Adopted Specification, Document ptc/03-10-04.

[OMG03b]   Object Management Group, Inc. *OCL 2.0*, October 2003. OMG Final Adopted Specification, Document ptc/03-10-14.

[OMG03c]   Object Management Group, Inc. *OMG Unified Modeling Language Specification, Version 1.5*, March 2003. OMG Document formal/03-03-01.

[OMG03d]   Object Management Group, Inc. *Unified Modeling Language: Superstructure, version 2.0*, August 2003. OMG Final Adopted Specification, Document ptc/03-08-02.

[OMG03e]   Object Management Group, Inc. *Unified Modeling Language (UML) Specification: Infrastructure, version 2.0*, December 2003. OMG Final Adopted Specification, Document ptc/03-09-15.

[Par72]   David L. Parnas. On the criteria to be used in decomposing systems into modules. *Communications of the ACM*, 15(12):1053–1058, 1972.

[Par76]   David L. Parnas. On the design and development of program families. *IEEE Transactions on Software Engineering*, SE-2(1):1–9, March 1976.

[PK99]   Wolfgang Pree and Kai Koskimies. Framelets – small is beautiful. In Mohamed E.
             Fayad, Douglas C. Schmidt, and Ralph E. Johnson, editors, *Building Application
             Frameworks: Object-Oriented Foundations of Framework Design*, pages 411–414.
             John Wiley & Sons, Inc., New York City, 1999.

[PK00]   Wolfgang Pree and Kai Koskimies. Framelets — small and loosely coupled
             frameworks. In Mohamed Fayad, editor, *ACM Computing Survey Symposium on
             Application Frameworks*, volume 32 issue 1es, pages 57–61. ACM Press, March
             2000.

[PP00]   Alessandro Pasetti and Wolfgang Pree. A reusable architecture for satellite
             control software. In *IEEE/AIAA 19th Digital Avionics Systems Conference
             (DASC2000)*, pages 7–13, Philadelphia, PA, October 2000.

[PP01]   Alessandro Pasetti and Wolfgang Pree. Embedded software market transforma-
             tion through reusable frameworks. In *EmSoft 2001: First Workshop on Embed-
             ded Software*, pages 8–10, Lake Tahoe, California, October 2001.

[PP04]   Gustav Pomberger and Wolfgang Pree. *Software Engineering*. Carl Hanser
             Verlag, September 2004. In German language.

[PPSS95]   Wolfgang Pree, Gustav Pomberger, Albert Schappert, and Peter Sommerlad.
             Active guidance of framework development. *Software — Concepts and Tools*,
             16:94–103, 1995.

[Pre95]   Wolfgang Pree. *Design patterns for object-oriented software development*. ACM
             Press / Addison-Wesley Publishing Co., 1995.

[Pre99]   Wolfgang Pree. Hot-spot-driven framework development. In Mohamed E. Fayad,
             Douglas C. Schmidt, and Ralph E. Johnson, editors, *Building Application Frame-
             works: Object-Oriented Foundations of Framework Design*, chapter 16, pages
             379–394. John Wiley & Sons, Inc., New York City, 1999.

[PRST99]   David Parsons, Awais Rashid, Andreas Speck, and Alexandru Telea. A "frame-
             work" for object oriented frameworks design. In *Proceedings of the Technology
             of Object-Oriented Languages and Systems (TOOLS 29)*, pages 141–152. IEEE
             Computer Society, 1999.

[Rat05]   IBM Rational website, 2005. Available online: `http://www-306.ibm.com/
             software/rational/` (cited 2005-02-22).

[RG98]   Dirk Riehle and Thomas Gross. Role model based framework design and integration. In *Proceedings of the 1998 Conference on Object-Oriented Programming Systems, Languages, and Applications (OOPSLA'98)*, pages 117–133. ACM Press, 1998.

[Rob99]   Jason Elliot Robbins. *Cognitive Support Features for Software Development Tools*. PhD d issertation, University of California, Irvine, USA, 1999.

[SA02]   Yasunobu Sanada and Rolf Adams. Representing design patterns and frameworks in UML — towards a comprehensive approach. *Journal of Object Technology*, 1(2):143–154, July-August 2002.

[Ski01]   Martin Skinner. Enhancing an open source UML editor by context-based constraints for components. Master's thesis, Technische Universität Berlin, Germany, December 2001.

[SWE04]   IEEE Computer Society. SWEBOK — Guide to the Software Engineering Body of Knowledge., 2004.

[TDK04]   TDL Development Kit (TDK), May 2004. Available online: `http://www.modecs.cc/results/software/TDK.zip` (cited 2005-03-18).

[Tem04a]   Josef Templ. TDL Specification and Report. Technical report, Department of Computer Science, University of Salzburg, Austria, March 2004. Available online: `http://www.softwareresearch.net/site/publications/C059.pdf` (cited 2005-03-18).

[Tem04b]   Josef Templ. TDL Tutorial. Tutorial, Department of Computer Science, University of Salzburg, Austria, June 2004. Available online as part of [TDK04].

[Tem04c]   Josef Templ. The Time Definition Language (TDL). Lecture notes for a course on distributed systems, 2004. Available online: `http://www.softwareresearch.net/site/teaching/WS0405/ds/docs/TDL.pdf` (cited 2005-03-18).

[Vil01]   Antti Viljamaa. *Pattern-Based Framework Annotation and Adaption — A Systematic Approach*. Licentiate thesis, Department of Computer Science, University of Helsinki, Finland, June 2001.

[WBM02]   Rebecca Wirfs-Brock and Alan McKean. The art of writing use cases. Tutorial at the 17th Annual ACM Conference on Object-Oriented Programming, Systems, Languages, and Applications (OOPSLA'02), November 2002.

[YA01]   Sherif M. Yacoub and Hany H. Ammar. UML support for designing software sys-
           tems as a composition of design patterns. In *UML '01: Proceedings of the 4th In-
           ternational Conference on The Unified Modeling Language, Modeling Languages,
           Concepts, and Tools*, Toronto, Ontario, Canada, October 2001. Springer-Verlag.

[ZJF03]   Tewfik Ziadi, Jean-Marc. Jézéquel, and Frédéric Fondement. Product line engi-
           neering with UML. Under submission. Available online: `http://www.esi.es/`
           `en/Projects/Families/famDissemination.html` (cited 2005-02-08), Septem-
           ber 2003.

VDM
Verlag
Dr. Müller

Wissenschaftlicher Buchverlag bietet

kostenfreie

Publikation

von

wissenschaftlichen Arbeiten

Diplomarbeiten, Magisterarbeiten, Master und Bachelor Theses
sowie Dissertationen, Habilitationen und wissenschaftliche Monographien

Sie verfügen über eine wissenschaftliche Abschlußarbeit zu aktuellen oder zeitlosen
Fragestellungen, die hohen inhaltlichen und formalen Ansprüchen genügt,
und haben **Interesse an einer honorarvergüteten Publikation**?

Dann senden Sie bitte erste Informationen über Ihre Arbeit per Email
an info@vdm-verlag.de. Unser Außenlektorat meldet sich umgehend bei Ihnen.

VDM Verlag Dr. Müller Aktiengesellschaft & Co. KG
Dudweiler Landstraße 125a
D - 66123 Saarbrücken

www.vdm-verlag.de

www.ingramcontent.com/pod-product-compliance
Lightning Source LLC
Chambersburg PA
CBHW071423050326
40689CB00010B/1963